WEST VIRGINIA WILDLIFE VIEWING GUIDE

by Mark Damian Duda

FALCON
HELENA MONTANA

Design, typesetting, and other prepress work by Falcon® Publishing,
Helena, Montana.

Printed in Korea.
1 2 3 4 5 6 7 8 9 0 CE 03 02 01 00 99

Defenders of Wildlife and its design are registered marks
of Defenders of Wildlife, Washington, D.C.

Watchable Wildlife® is a registered trademark of Falcon Publishing.

Library of Congress Cataloging-in-Publication Data

Duda, Mark Damian.
    West Virginia wildlife viewing guide / by Mark Duda.
        p. cm.
    Includes index.
    ISBN 1-56044-635-8 (pbk. : alk. paper)
    1. Wildlife viewing sites—West Virginia—Guidebooks. 2. Wildlife
    watching—West Virginia—Guidebooks. 3. West Virginia—Guidebooks.
    I. Title.
QL213.D84 1998
591.9754—dc21   98-26968
                                                              CIP

Front cover photo
River otter, by Jim Roetzel

Back cover photos
Box turtle, by Jim Clark
New River Gorge, by Stephen J. Shaluta Jr.

Illustrations
Todd Telander

Greetings from the Governor:

Throughout my life, I have enjoyed spending time in the great outdoors of West Virginia. We are truly blessed in West Virginia with awe-inspiring natural beauty and spectacular scenery unmatched anywhere in America. Clearly, the state's wildlife resources add greatly to the quality of the environment we all enjoy. With the publication of this guide and the creation of the state's wildlife viewing areas, we invite you to share the enjoyment of these resources with us.

When I was governor during my first term 40 years ago, much of West Virginia's charm was cut off from the rest of the world because our winding roads were too challenging for potential visitors. Today, tourism is our fastest growing industry, and West Virginia is now just a short drive from many major cities.

The Mountain State is rich with natural resources, and our wildlife is diverse and plentiful. As a result, West Virginians have a special relationship with fish and wildlife, making these resources an important part of the cultural and recreational activities of everyday life in our state.

Fish and wildlife are also an important part of West Virginia's economy. Each year, hunters, anglers, photographers, naturalists, and bird watchers spend nearly 14 million visitor days here and contribute about $820 million to the state's economy while they pursue various recreational activities related to wildlife resources.

Wildlife in West Virginia is for everyone, and we invite you to use this guide to add to your knowledge and enjoyment of the Mountain State's rich wildlife heritage. I hope you will use it often and come to appreciate West Virginia's great outdoors as I have.

Very sincerely,

Cecil H. Underwood

ABOUT THE WEST VIRGINIA DIVISION OF
NATURAL RESOURCES

The West Virginia Division of Natural Resources, Wildlife Resources Section is responsible for the management of all fish and wildlife within the State of West Virginia, a 24,231-square-mile area. Species are managed not only for their recreational value, but for scientific study and educational values. The Division's wildlife resources mission is mandated in state law:

> *It is declared to be the public policy of the State of West Virginia that the wildlife resources of this State shall be protected for the use and enjoyment of all the citizens of this State. All species of wildlife shall be maintained for values which may be either intrinsic or ecological or of benefit to man. Such benefits shall include (1) hunting, fishing, and other diversified recreational uses; (2) economic contributions in the best interest of the people of this State; and (3) scientific and educational uses.*

The Wildlife Resources Section manages the State's wildlife resources through the following major programmatic areas: cold water fisheries; warm water fisheries; wildlife; and special projects, planning, and biometrics. The Section has a staff of approximately 200 and operates from eight major offices across the state of West Virginia through six administrative districts. These program areas cover the diverse wildlife resources of the Mountain State from white-tailed deer to the Cheat Mountain salamander.

The Wildlife Resources Section is responsible for wildlife and fisheries management on approximately 400,000 acres of state-owned land and another one million acres of federally owned land through cooperative agreements. An extensive effort is also made by the Section to provide fishing and boating access to the state's streams and lakes.

As you visit West Virginia you are urged to visit our offices and obtain information about the State's public lands and fishing and boating access sites.

This guide is the first step for the West Virginia Wildlife Resources Section's Watchable Wildlife Program. The development of this guide has been made possible through a cooperative effort between the Wildlife Resources Section; the West Virginia Department of Transportation; and the U.S. Department of Transportation, Federal Highway Administration through an ISTEA grant.

U.S. Department
of Transportation

ABOUT THE WEST VIRGINIA DEPARTMENT OF TRANSPORTATION'S DIVISION OF HIGHWAYS

The West Virginia Department of Transportation's Division of Highways is responsible for planning, construction, and maintenance of a modern, safe, and efficient transportation system for the State of West Virginia. The wealth of abundant recreational resources in West Virginia is accessible from a growing and improving network of interstate and Appalachian Corridor highways, as well as the state's scenic "Country Roads."

WVDOT and the Federal Highway Administration are proud to have provided funding for this Wildlife Viewing Guide through a Transportation Enhancement Grant.

Transportation Secretary Samuel G. Bonasso invites everyone to visit the Mountain State, drive safely, and come again.

ACKNOWLEDGMENTS

This book was made possible by the commitment and perseverance of Kathy Leo, Nongame Project Leader, West Virginia Division of Natural Resources, Wildlife Resources Section. Kathy assisted in all phases of this book, including initiating, planning, and writing grants for funding this project. Gordon Robertson, Deputy Chief, Wildlife Resources Section, also played a critical role in the initiation, development, and completion of this guide. Without their commitment to wildlife conservation and enhancement of wildlife viewing opportunities in West Virginia, this book would not exist.

We are also indebted to Bernard F. Dowler, Chief, Wildlife Resources Section; Charles B. Felton, Jr., former Director, Division of Natural Resources; Fred VanKirk, former Secretary, Commissioner of Highways; and Kate Davies, Viewing Guide Program Manager, Defenders of Wildlife, for their assistance and unswerving commitment to the production of this book.

The following individuals provided invaluable assistance, important information, experience, and expertise for this guide: Angel Adams, Mary Beth Adams, Ernest Adkins, David S. Alt, Richard Backus, Steven P. Bolar, Ed Boyd, Dr. George Breiding, Barbara Breshock, Melissa Brown, Janet Butler, J. Scott Butterworth, Jim Clark, Mark Clark, Bill Compton, Keith Cooper, Janet Corbitt, Tom Dale, Tammy Davis, Julius Davidson, A. Scott Durham, Bob Eakin, Laura Earles, Charles E. Ellison, Theresa Evans, Ronald E. Fawcett, Nancy Feakes, Mark Fitzpatrick, Mark Ford, Don Gasper, Bernard Gibson, Dr. Tina Hall, C. J. Hamilton, Christopher Scott Hannah, Rich Hartman, John Hendley, Wilbur L. Hershberger, Larry Hines, Pat Hissom, Eugene A. Holland II, Emily Hudok, Bill Igo, Frank Jernejcic, Paul Johansen, Daniel B. Johnson, L. Johnson, Debbie Keener, Al Kerns, Keith Krantz, Jeff Layfield, Cass Matthew, Dr. Ed Michael, Katy Miller, David McClung, Jeffrey W. McCrady, Allan Niederberger, Bert Nolan, John Northeimer, Susan Olcott, Jesse Overcash, Ford Parker, Dale Pase, Harry Pawelczyk, Wendy Perrone, Donald Phares, Jim Phillips, Steve Rauch, Calvin Redman, Brad Reed, Dr. Dave Samuel, Jo Santiago, Sara Schell, Bill Schiffer, Lynette Serlin, Kem Shaw, Don Shenefiel, Thomas L. Shriver, Ken Shugart, Rob Silvester, R. Keith Simmons, David A. Smith, Dan Talbot, Dr. Linda Thomasma, Gene Thorn, Homer Tinney, William E. Vanscoy, Jo Wargo, Barry Warhoftig, Jonathan Weems, Bill Wylie, Lynne Wiseman, Doug Wood, and Matt Yeager.

CONTENTS

AN INTRODUCTION TO THE MOUNTAIN STATE

West Virginia means wildlands, and wildlands mean wildlife. From the wind-swept Allegheny Mountains in the east to the Ohio River in the west, West Virginia is home to 67 species of mammals, 176 species of fish, 299 species of birds, 43 species of amphibians, and 42 species of reptiles. More than 128 butterfly species grace the skies, and 2,300 species of vascular plants blanket the rugged landscape. West Virginia, the Mountain State, is the most elevated state east of the Mississippi River, with a mean elevation of 1,500 feet. With raging whitewater rivers, vast expanses of designated wilderness areas, one of the deepest gorges in the eastern United States, and the second oldest river in the world, it is no wonder West Virginia is often referred to as "wild and wonderful."

The state's extensive and diverse system of public lands and preserves offers outdoor enthusiasts and wildlife viewers a wide range of opportunities. West Virginia has 66 public wildlife management areas, 9 state forests, and more than 200,000 acres of state parks. The nation's 500th national wildlife refuge was created in 1994 at Canaan Valley. One hundred thousand acres of the George Washington National Forest straddle the Virginia–West Virginia border in Hampshire, Hardy, and Pendleton counties, and 18,211 acres of the Jefferson National

Forest are located in Monroe County. At almost one million acres, the Monongahela National Forest dominates the Potomac highlands region in the east. The West Virginia chapter of The Nature Conservancy has protected 29,000 acres and owns and manages 23 nature preserves throughout West Virginia. The corporate sector is working to conserve wildlife as well, as seen at the PPG Industries–Natrium Plant Wildlife Project, where wildlife viewing opportunities range from auto tours to isolated islands accessible only by boat.

This guide showcases some of the best places in West Virginia to view wild animals in their natural habitat. Almost 200 sites were considered, and stringent standards were used to evaluate the 63 viewing sites that made the cut. Many worthy sites were not included due to space limitations; others were eliminated to protect fragile wildlife and habitats from damage.

Before visiting a site, carefully review the information presented in this guide for the types of wildlife found in a specific area, the optimal seasons for viewing selected species, on-site facilities, special attractions, and viewing tips designed to help you see more wildlife. Use the wealth of information presented in this guide, and your chances for a successful wildlife viewing trip will be dramatically increased. Be sure to travel with an up-to-date road atlas. Obtain a free West Virginia map by phoning 1-800-CALL-WVA. Or purchase the indispensable *DeLorme West Virginia Atlas & Gazetteer*, which includes detailed topographic maps of the entire state. DeLorme maps are available in many West Virginia stores.

So pack up your binoculars, identification guides, and cameras, lace up your hiking boots, and head out to one of the 63 great sites highlighted in the *West Virginia Wildlife Viewing Guide*.

Hawk watching, Dolly Sods.

HOW TO USE THIS GUIDE

This guide is divided into four sections, representing the principal biophysical regions of West Virginia. At the beginning of each section, wildlife viewing sites are listed and located on a map. The text for each viewing site includes the following elements, which describe and interpret the habitats and the wildlife you may see. Pay attention to NOTES OF CAUTION in capital letters.

Description: Briefly explains the area, facilities, and wildlife.

Viewing information: Expands on the site description, providing the seasonal likelihood of spotting wildlife along with other interesting information about the area. May include details about access and parking.

Directions: *Provides written directions for each site. Supplement this information with an up-to-date West Virginia road map or a West Virginia Atlas and Gazetteer.*

Ownership: Includes the name of the agency, organization, or company that owns or manages the site. The telephone number listed may be used to obtain more information.

Recreation and facility icons: Indicates some of the facilities and opportunities available at each site. The managing agency or organization can provide more information and describe other types of opportunities available.

FACILITIES AND RECREATION

Entry or Use Fee	Parking	Restrooms	Barrier-Free	Restaurant	Picnic Area	Lodging

Camping	Hiking	Bicycling	Boat Ramp	Large Boats	Small Boats

WEST VIRGINIA
WILDLIFE VIEWING AREAS

This guide is divided into four principal biophysical regions or sections, as shown on this map. Each chapter of this book covers one of the four regions. A detailed regional map appears at the beginning of each chapter.

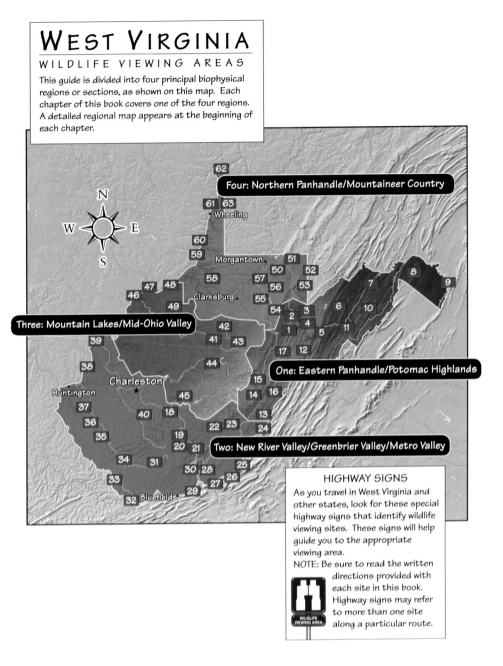

Four: Northern Panhandle/Mountaineer Country

Three: Mountain Lakes/Mid-Ohio Valley

One: Eastern Panhandle/Potomac Highlands

Two: New River Valley/Greenbrier Valley/Metro Valley

HIGHWAY SIGNS

As you travel in West Virginia and other states, look for these special highway signs that identify wildlife viewing sites. These signs will help guide you to the appropriate viewing area.

NOTE: Be sure to read the written directions provided with each site in this book. Highway signs may refer to more than one site along a particular route.

THE NATIONAL WATCHABLE WILDLIFE PROGRAM

The National Watchable Wildlife Program is a nationwide cooperative effort to combine wildlife conservation with America's growing interest in wildlife-related outdoor recreation. The concept of the program is simple: People want to watch wildlife, and they want to watch wildlife in natural settings. But they don't always know where to go, they don't know when to go, and they don't know what to expect when they get there. The National Watchable Wildlife Program is designed to answer those needs. Each participating state identifies its best places for viewing wildlife; a uniform system of road signs (the binoculars logo you see on the cover of this guide) is put in place to help direct travelers; and guidebooks like this one give wildlife enthusiasts specific information about the sites.

Though license fees and taxes paid by hunters and anglers have primarily helped fund wildlife conservation and recreation in the past, additional sources of revenue are required for increased conservation efforts. Efforts are underway at state and national levels to develop new funding mechanisms.

In West Virginia, the Watchable Wildlife Program has been organized by the state Division of Natural Resources with funding from the state Department of Transportation and the Federal Highway Administration. As time goes on, sites will be enhanced with trails, viewing blinds, and platforms, and interpretive material such as signs, bird and animal lists, and brochures.

The goal of the Watchable Wildlife Program is to make wildlife viewing fun. But in a larger context, the Watchable Wildlife Program is about conservation. It began in 1990 with the signing of a Memorandum of Understanding by eight federal land management agencies, the International Association of Fish and Wildlife Agencies, and four national conservation groups. The program is founded on the notion that, given opportunities to enjoy and learn about wildlife in natural settings, people will become advocates for conservation in the future. **The success of wildlife conservation everywhere depends on the interest and active involvement of citizens.**

The *West Virginia Wildlife Viewing Guide* is the 28th book in the Watchable Wildlife series that forms the cornerstone of the program. Each of the sites mentioned in this book is marked with the brown-and-white binocular logo. Similar viewing networks have been established in more than half of the 50 states. Thus, the effort is part of a growing nationwide network.

Use this guide to make your wildlife watching trips fun and successful, use it to discover West Virginia in new ways, and as you travel around West Virginia, remember these places can only exist with the support of interested citizens like you. Support conservation efforts in every way you can.

STEPS TO SUCCESSFUL WILDLIFE VIEWING

Wildlife is often closer and more abundant than you might think. Here are five basic steps to increase your chances of seeing wildlife:

1. Look in the right place.
2. Look at the right time.
3. Develop wildlife viewing skills and techniques.
4. Understand the species and its habits.
5. Follow the wildlife watchers code of ethics.

Research shows that wildlife watching is one of the best environmental education tools available. Children who watch wildlife in its natural habitat know more about wildlife and hold more realistic attitudes toward wildlife than children who learn about wildlife only through television, zoos, or lectures.

STEP 1: LOOK IN THE RIGHT PLACE

If you want to see certain animals, you need to find out where—exactly—they live. Each species is found only in a certain geographic area, known as its range. Some species, such as white-tailed deer, have a large range and are found throughout West Virginia. Other species have a much more limited range. The midland smooth softshell turtle is known to occur in only one county in West Virginia, Mason County, along the Ohio River. The range of the rough green snake is western and central West Virginia, while the range of the eastern smooth green snake is in the mountainous region of the eastern part of the state.

Within its range, the species lives within a specific habitat. A habitat is a place its provides the right combination of food, water, and cover a species needs for nesting, hiding, feeding, and sleeping. Habitat needs can vary greatly from one species to the next, even when the animals seem similar. Consider the red-tailed hawk and the red-shouldered hawk. To judge from their names, you might think these two birds are nearly identical. However, red-shouldered hawks prefer to live in swampy woods where they feed mostly on snakes and frogs. Red-tailed hawks favor drier, open areas, such as fields and pasturelands, and feed mostly on small rodents. They prefer different habitats.

Location is also an important consideration if you want to see migrating hawks and eagles in the fall. During migration, these birds of prey follow West Virginia's ridges and wind currents southward. The best viewing locales are mountaintops where the geography and wind currents are just right, such as at Cold Knob Scenic Area (site 23), Hanging Rock Raptor Migration Observatory (site 26), and the Allegheny Front Migration Observatory located at Dolly Sods (site 5).

Recognizing the link between a species and its habitat is a fundamental lesson in successful wildlife viewing. It is also a lesson in wildlife conservation. Without proper habitat, a wildlife species cannot exist. Habitat destruction and alteration are two of the greatest threats to North America's wildlife.

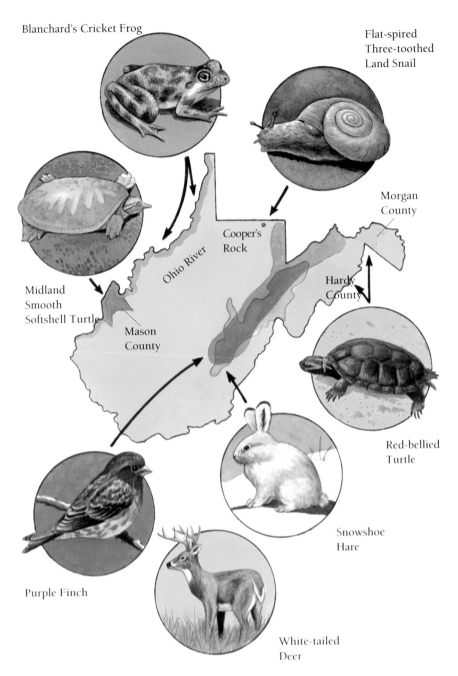

Blanchard's Cricket Frog

Flat-spired Three-toothed Land Snail

Morgan County

Cooper's Rock

Ohio River

Hardy County

Midland Smooth Softshell Turtle

Mason County

Red-bellied Turtle

Purple Finch

Snowshoe Hare

White-tailed Deer

Each species is found only in a certain geographic area, known as its range. Within that range, the species lives within a specific habitat.

STEP 2: LOOK AT THE RIGHT TIME

Timing is everything. Animal activity depends on the time of day and the time of year. Some animals, such as songbirds, hawks, wild turkeys, and red and gray squirrels, are active during the day (diurnal). Other species, such as owls, bats, raccoons, flying squirrels, and opossums, are active at night (nocturnal).

In general, early morning and evening are the best times to view most birds and large mammals, since they are most active at these times. At midday, watch for hawks "kettling," circling and soaring on columns of rising warm air. You don't have to limit your wildlife experiences to daytime hours, however. At night, listen for owls or whip-poor-wills. Also, some wildlife watchers use night-vision viewers to open up a whole new world of wildlife viewing. Originally designed for military and law enforcement use, night-vision viewers are used by wildlife viewers to open up the nocturnal world and find previously unseen wildlife.

Some wildlife species are present in West Virginia only during certain times of the year, or they hibernate and can't be seen during the winter months. Thirty-nine species of wood warblers occur in West Virginia—but only in the spring and summer. These small, brightly colored birds winter in the Caribbean and Central and South America, hence the term, "neotropical migratory songbirds." Some animals appear only at certain times of the year, but not because they migrate. These animals are out of sight because they hibernate, or become inactive during the winter season. The Eastern pipistrelle, one of the more common bats in West Virginia, hibernates in caves during the winter. Though not true hibernators, black bears do become inactive during cold weather.

Another timing issue to consider is weather. Changes in weather can present wildlife viewing opportunities. After rain, many predators emerge to feed on displaced insects and rodents. Wetter, cooler weather associated with low-pressure systems can increase your chance of seeing animals.

Many animals are active just after a storm, and wildlife seem less sensitive to noise and smell at that time. Cold fronts often "push" migrating birds south in the fall. Time your trips to one of West Virginia's mountaintops in the fall after one of these cold fronts to see migrating hawks and eagles.

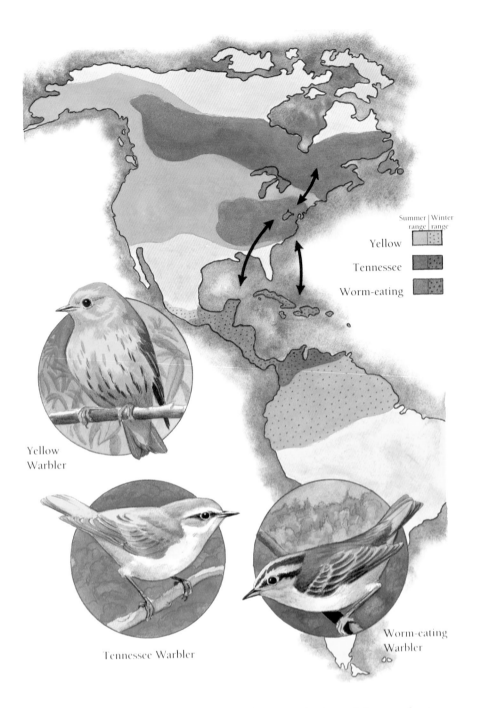

Summer | Winter
range | range

Yellow

Tennessee

Worm-eating

Yellow
Warbler

Tennessee Warbler

Worm-eating
Warbler

Many species are found in West Virginia only at certain times of the year due to migration.

STEP 3: DEVELOP WILDLIFE VIEWING SKILLS AND TECHNIQUES

Developing sharp senses is the first step to seeing more animals in the field. Try to really focus your eyes and tune your ears. Many animals camouflage themselves, blending into the environment, so you'll need to look at more than the obvious. Try the following:

- Look for subtle movements in bushes, shrubs, and trees.
- Make "owl eyes" by making an "okay" sign with your hand, bringing the rest of your fingers into the circle, then looking through them. This helps focus your attention.
- Look for parts of an animal, rather than its entire body.
- Cup your hands around your ears to amplify sounds.
- Look above and below you. Wildlife can be seen in many different layers—in the sky, in the treetops, in the understory, and beneath your feet.

Use these strategies to get closer to wildlife:

- Use optics. Binoculars and spotting scopes are two good ways to get close to wildlife.
- Use a blind. A blind is anything that conceals you from the animals that you want to observe. Blinds may include your vehicle, boxes, homemade blinds, even fancy, portable, commercial blinds similar to a pop-up tent. Blinds are used because some animals, such as waterfowl, have excellent eyesight, and blinds conceal your movement.
- Use a vehicle as a blind. Many animals have become habituated to vehicles; they don't seem to be afraid of them and will often approach or pass right by your car. Turn your engine off, sit quietly in your vehicle and wait for wildlife to come to you. If you need to shift around inside your vehicle, move slowly. Do not get out when animals are near—you'll send them off in panic. If you see animals while your car is running, don't turn your engine off, since this will also panic them.
- Sit still. Find a comfortable place, sit down, relax, and remain still. Most animals' eyes are made to detect motion. Lean up against a tree to break your silhouette. Trees and vegetation make great viewing blinds. If you wear dark-colored clothes or camouflage and use a dropcloth of camouflage netting, you'll increase the odds of going unnoticed. If you sit absolutely still, you will also see animals reappear because they think you have gone.
- Walk quietly and slowly. Few animals walk with the steady gait that humans do. Break your natural pattern; take a few steps, avoid brittle sticks or leaves, then stop, look, and listen. Walk into the wind whenever possible, since many animals have an excellent sense of smell. If you cross a stream, look upstream and downstream since often the sound of flowing water will deaden your noise and the animal will not realize you are close.
- Look for animal sign. Tracks in the mud or snow, vegetation that has been recently browsed, and scat are all clues to help find animals, or at least to appreciate them while they're out of sight.

When it comes to wildlife viewing, patience in the field pays off, as these two mountaineers have discovered.

- Use field guides. Many good field guides are available to help identify mammals, birds, fish, and other fauna and flora. Knowing what you're looking at greatly enhances your viewing pleasure.
- Ask an expert. Several of the viewing areas have on-site staff. Don't be afraid to ask for advice. It can often make the difference between a disappointing visit and one you will remember forever.
- Be patient. Allow yourself enough time in the field. There is a relationship between the amount of time you are in the field and the amount of wildlife you see.

STEP 4: UNDERSTAND WILDLIFE SPECIES AND THEIR HABITS

It's important to understand the species and the habits of the species you are looking for or looking at. This will give you a better appreciation of exactly what you are seeing, and will assist you in field identification. When viewing an animal, observe its colors, shape, "field marks," and behavior. Hone your skills in identifying different species, and notice the difference between male and female animals, as well as between younger animals and older ones. For example, although the Kentucky warbler and the common yellowthroat, two common wood warblers in West Virginia in summer, look somewhat similar, the Kentucky warbler has distinctive yellow patches, like spectacles, around its eyes. Female belted kingfishers have brown breastbands while males do not. Juvenile bald eagles lack the distinctive white head and tail so characteristic of adult birds.

Behavior can be used to distinguish the two major duck groups: dabbling or puddle ducks such as mallard, pintail, wood duck, and black duck; and diving ducks, including bufflehead, mergansers, and common goldeneye. Dabbling ducks feed by tipping underwater for grasses and plant seeds. They take flight directly from the water. Diving ducks submerge to eat small fish, crustaceans, mollusks, and aquatic plants. They must "patter" along the water to gain speed before taking flight.

STEP 5: FOLLOW THE WILDLIFE WATCHER'S CODE OF ETHICS

Your goal as a wildlife watcher is to observe and enjoy wild animals in their natural habitat without interrupting their normal behavior or disturbing their habitat. Overzealous viewers can cause serious problems for the very animals they care so much about. Too often, wildlife watchers tend to think of their own behavior during a single encounter with an animal, not of the cumulative impacts of previous wildlife watchers. For the well-being of wildlife, however, viewers must consider the impact of all those human-wildlife encounters that preceded their visit, and all those that will follow. Give wildlife plenty of space. Binoculars and spotting scopes allow you to view wildlife without getting too close. Approach wildlife slowly, quietly, and indirectly. Always give animals an avenue for retreat. Be respectful of nesting and denning areas and rookeries. Well-meaning but intrusive visitors may cause parents to flee, leaving their young vulnerable to the elements or predators. Stay on designated trails whenever possible. Leave "orphaned" or sick animals alone. Young animals that appear

Let an animal's behavior help you identify it. These wildlife viewers can be sure these wood ducks are "puddle ducks" because they take flight directly from the water.

alone usually have parents waiting nearby. Restrain pets or leave them at home. They may startle, chase, or even kill wildlife. Learn to recognize signs of alarm. These are sometimes subtle, but leave if an animal shows them.

And finally, don't feed the wildlife. Sharing food can get animals hooked on handouts; it may even harm their digestive systems. Animals that are fed learn to associate people with food and often approach vehicles, increasing their chances of being hit. Also, animals that are fed by humans are more likely to become victims of poaching. It's also illegal to feed some species.

Boardwalks help protect fragile wetland ecosystems.

A good pair of binoculars helps you get closer to wild animals without disturbing them.

Black bear yearling. BILL LEA PHOTO

REGION ONE: EASTERN PANHANDLE/ POTOMAC HIGHLANDS

Characterized by the Mountain State's highest elevations, deep forested valleys, and almost a million acres of public lands, the Eastern Panhandle/ Potomac Highlands Region is one of the top wildlife viewing destinations in the East. The Allegheny Mountains, oriented northeast-southwest, dominate the landscape, and the protected wildlands here provide important habitat for black bears, wild turkeys, and numerous reptiles and amphibians. Spot snowshoe hare in their white pelage in winter, exquisitely colored warblers in the spring, and white-tailed deer by the dozens in a meadow in summer. In fall, climb to a rocky peak and watch for migrating hawks, including red-tailed, Cooper's, broad-winged, sharp-shinned, and others.

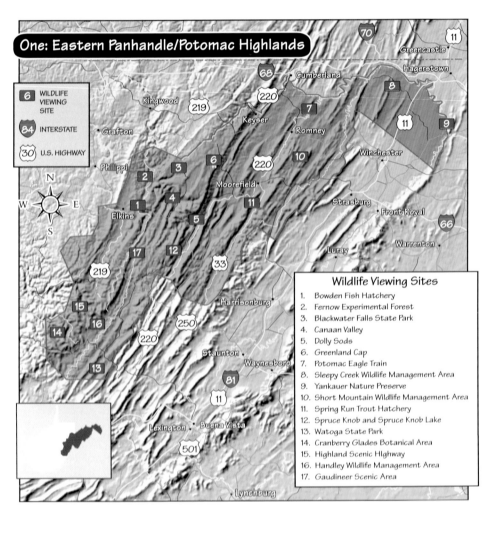

One: Eastern Panhandle/Potomac Highlands

6 WILDLIFE VIEWING SITE

84 INTERSTATE

30 U.S. HIGHWAY

Wildlife Viewing Sites

1. Bowden Fish Hatchery
2. Fernow Experimental Forest
3. Blackwater Falls State Park
4. Canaan Valley
5. Dolly Sods
6. Greenland Cap
7. Potomac Eagle Train
8. Sleepy Creek Wildlife Management Area
9. Yankauer Nature Preserve
10. Short Mountain Wildlife Management Area
11. Spring Run Trout Hatchery
12. Spruce Knob and Spruce Knob Lake
13. Watoga State Park
14. Cranberry Glades Botanical Area
15. Highland Scenic Highway
16. Handley Wildlife Management Area
17. Gaudineer Scenic Area

1. BOWDEN FISH HATCHERY

Description: Formerly called the Bowden National Fish Hatchery, this hatchery was acquired by the state in 1997 and is now managed by the Wildlife Resources Section. Bowden annually produces 160,000 pounds of brook, brown, rainbow, and golden rainbow trout, which are stocked into West Virginia waters.

Viewing Information: Bowden offers wildlife viewers the chance to see fish hatchery operations firsthand, and to get a close look at the trout that inhabit West Virginia's waters. Tour the visitor center, open from June to October, the hatchery building where up to two million trout eggs can be incubated, and the concrete "raceways" where larger fish are held.

Directions: *From Elkins, travel east on U.S. Highway 33 for 3 miles. Turn left off US 33 onto Old Route 33 (US 33-8), and proceed for 5 miles to the hatchery (on the right).*

Ownership: West Virginia Division of Natural Resources (304) 637-0238

Size: 35 acres   **Closest Town:** Elkins

Trout are kept indoors at hatcheries until they are three to four inches in length. At that time they are moved to these pools or "raceways" until they are stocked in West Virginia waters. BOWDEN FISH HATCHERY PHOTO

2. FERNOW EXPERIMENTAL FOREST

Description: The Fernow is located in one of the most mountainous regions of the Mountain State, and is an active research forest. The purpose of this experimental forest is to foster a better understanding of West Virginia's forests, water, soils, and wildlife resources in order to protect and conserve these valuable resources. This research area was carved from the Monongahela National Forest in 1934 because it is representative of many of West Virginia's forests.

Viewing Information: Although the Fernow is fairly small at 4,700 acres, it is highly diverse, well roaded, and provides numerous wildlife viewing opportunities. The forest is an excellent place to see neotropical migratory songbirds in the spring and summer. White-tailed deer, ruffed grouse, wild turkeys, and several species of squirrel are present, as are black bears. The amphibian and reptile populations are diverse. Salamanders include redback, spotted, mountain dusky, Appalachian seal, slimy, Wehrle's, four-toed, northern spring, northern red, and northern two-lined. The Appalachian seal salamander can be found during the day under rocks in cool mountain streams. The slimy salamander is active at night or in the afternoon following warm rains. The four-toed salamander prefers hardwood forests, but during spring, females migrate to bogs to deposit eggs. Fernow staff provide "show-me" trips, which provide a lecturer or a guided tour through the forest. Contact the Timber and Watershed Laboratory, Nursery Bottom, Parsons, WV, 26287, or phone 304-478-2000. THIS IS A PUBLIC HUNTING AREA; PLEASE CHECK WITH THE MANAGER FOR SEASONS AND AFFECTED AREAS. THE FERNOW IS AN ACTIVE RESEARCH FOREST, PLEASE DO NOT DISTURB THE FOREST.

Directions: *At the junction of U.S. Highway 219 and West Virginia State Route 72 in Parsons follow US 219 north 0.2 mile (just over the bridge) to the sign for Otter Creek Wilderness. Turn right and then make an immediate left (the road is not marked). Proceed 1.3 miles to the fork and bear left; there will be a sign for Fernow Forest. Travel 1 mile to the fork and bear right at the sign for Forest Road 701. Go 0.2 mile to the entrance.*

Ownership: USDA Forest Service (304) 478-2000

Size: 4,700 acres   **Closest Town:** Parsons

Bright yellow spots in two irregular rows covering a black body distinguish the spotted salamander.
LEONARD LEE RUE III PHOTO

3. BLACKWATER FALLS STATE PARK

Description: The centerpiece of this state park is the 62-foot-high Blackwater Falls, created as softer rock beneath the falls eroded faster than the harder caprock top, producing a ledge five stories high. The "blackwater" that flows over the falls and through the 8-mile-long, 525-foot-deep Blackwater Gorge, gets its amber color from leached tannic acids from fallen hemlock and red spruce needles. The diverse habitats here—northern coniferous forest, northern hardwood forest, and cranberry bogs—support numerous wildlife species.

Viewing Information: White-tailed deer are common and easily seen throughout the park. Other mammals here include black bears, seen between May and October in quieter sections of the park; striped skunks; gray and red foxes; woodland, meadow, and southern red-backed voles; white-footed and deer mice; muskrats; beavers; woodchucks; eastern cottontails; and several species of squirrels, including eastern gray, fox, red and southern flying. Red squirrels, also known as fairy diddles, prefer coniferous forests and are usually heard before seen. Listen for their scolding ratchetlike chatter as you walk along a trail, and then search the lower branches of the tree. Fox squirrels are the largest of the tree squirrels and prefer mature hardwood forests. The smaller eastern gray squirrel, a common sight in backyards and city parks throughout the state, has a bushy tail bordered with white-tipped hairs. The diminutive southern flying squirrel is nocturnal, usually appearing late in the evening, gliding from tree to tree. Songbird viewing is excellent in the park, especially in summer when many species of warblers can be seen, such as the magnolia and the black-throated green. Solitary and red-eyed vireos are common during the summer whereas black-capped chickadees, tufted titmice, eastern bluebirds, and golden-crowned kinglets are year-round residents.

Directions: From Davis, travel north on West Virginia State Route 32. Turn left off WV 32 onto County Route 29. Proceed south on CR 29 for 1 mile to the park entrance.

Ownership: West Virginia Division of Natural Resources (304) 259-5216

Size: 1,688 acres   **Closest Town:** Davis

Southern flying squirrels are West Virginia's smallest squirrel, weighing only 2 to 3 ounces. Their total length is 8 to 9 inches, which includes a 3- to 4-inch tail.
RON AUSTING PHOTO

4. CANAAN VALLEY

Description: Canaan Valley is the largest wetland complex in West Virginia and is the highest valley of its size east of the Rockies. It supports an incredible abundance of wildlife: 288 species of mammals, birds, reptiles, amphibians, and fish, and almost 600 different species of plants occur here. The valley is composed of an array of public and private land including Canaan Valley State Park, the nearby Dolly Sods Wilderness Area, Blackwater Falls State Park, and the nation's 500th national wildlife refuge, Canaan Valley National Wildlife Refuge.

Viewing Information: The most visible species here is the white-tailed deer. Hike any of the Canaan Valley State Park roads or numerous trails and look for deer in the many clearings early in the morning or early evening to see them feeding. Less visible because they are more active in the evening, but just as fun to observe is the semiaquatic mammal, the muskrat, which might be seen along the Abe Run Boardwalk and the Blackwater River Trail. Look for swamp sparrows and cedar waxwings along the boardwalk in spring, and in summer look for common yellowthroats, the males easily identified by their black face mask above the yellow throat. In summer search the forest and its edge for other migratory songbirds like indigo buntings, magnolia warblers, Blackburnian warblers, and hermit thrushes. Black bears have become more numerous here and are sometimes seen in spring and fall. Start your visit off right by picking up "A Guide to the Birds of Canaan Valley State Park and the Surrounding Area" at the Nature Center.

Directions: *From Davis, travel south on West Virginia State Route 32 for 13 miles. Canaan Valley Resort State Park entrance is on the right.*

Ownership: West Virginia Division of Natural Resources (304) 866-4111

Size: 6,015 acres   **Closest Town**: Davis

Wetland, Canaan Valley State Park. JIM CLARK PHOTO

29

Bear Rocks, Dolly Sods. JIM CLARK PHOTO

5. DOLLY SODS

Description: High elevation, sweeping open vistas, windswept rocks, and plains characterize this rugged area. The one-sided spruce trees are testimony to the fierce west winds that sweep through the heath barren plant community of this high plateau. Though the road to Dolly Sods is narrow and rough and some areas may be crowded at certain times of year, the patient visitor can enter a unique ecosystem rich in biodiversity.

Viewing Information: The Allegheny Front Migration Observatory is located opposite the entrance to Red Creek Campground and is a great place to begin your exploration of Dolly Sods. Between mid-August and mid-October during the early morning, this bird-banding station is an excellent place to view migrating songbirds and hawks. In mid-September the station is staffed, and biologists are usually available to answer questions about the site's bird netting and banding procedures. Visitors are likely to see several species of migrating warblers, including bay-breasted, Blackburnian, black-throated blue, black-throated green, blackpoll, Cape May, magnolia, and Tennessee, as well as common yellowthroats and Swainson's thrushes. This area is also one of the best places in West Virginia to see black bears. THIS IS A NATURAL AREA WITH FEW FACILITIES. PORTIONS OF THE ROUGH, UNPAVED ROAD THROUGH DOLLY SODS ARE CLOSED AT CERTAIN TIMES OF YEAR. PLEASE CHECK WITH THE MANAGER FOR SEASONAL CLOSURES. SOME AREAS ARE OPEN TO HUNTING; CHECK WITH THE MANAGER FOR SEASONS AND AFFECTED AREAS.

Directions: From Petersburg travel north on West Virginia State Route 42 approximately 12 miles to County Route 28-7 (Jordan Run Road/Hopeville Gap Road). Turn left off WV 42 onto CR 28-7 and travel south for 5.2 miles. Turn right onto Forest Road 75 and proceed for 4.7 miles.

Ownership: USDA Forest Service (304) 567-2827

Size: 10,215 acres   **Closest Town**: Petersburg

Blueberry bushes in Dolly Sods turn a brilliant scarlet in autumn.
STEPHEN J. SHALUTA JR. PHOTO

31

6. GREENLAND GAP

Description: Though small, this site has a lot to offer, including 800-foot cliffs that tower over a hemlock-draped, crystalline stream. Greenland Gap is one of 24 nature preserves owned and maintained by the West Virginia chapter of The Nature Conservancy.

Viewing Information: White-tailed deer, wild turkeys, and ruffed grouse are present year-round. May 5 through May 15 is usually the peak season for viewing migrating neotropical birds. Common ravens and turkey vultures nest here because the cliffs are an ideal place to lay eggs. Turkey vultures do not build nests, but simply place their two eggs in a crevice in rocks or in a fallen log. Ravens build nests out of sticks and line them with moss or lichens to lay their four to seven eggs. In summer explore the clear stream for fish and amphibians. In July, blooming rhododendrons fill the forest understory. After a cold front in the fall, several migrating birds of prey might be seen from the trail that leads to the top of the cliffs. THIS IS A NATURAL AREA WITH NO FACILITIES.

Directions: From Scherr, travel east on West Virginia State Route 93 for about 500 feet. Turn right off WV 93 onto County Route 1 (Greenland Road). Keep left on Greenland Road, cross the bridge, and go about 1 mile to the town of Greenland. Turn right on CR 3-3; do not continue straight on the gravel road. You will enter the area after about 0.3 mile; the main entrance sign, parking pullout, and trailhead are at the east end of the area on CR 3-3.

Ownership: The Nature Conservancy, West Virginia Chapter (304) 345-4350

Size: 250 acres   **Closest Town**: Scherr

A member of the heath family, the rhododendron is an evergreen shrub which forms dense thickets.
JIM CLARK PHOTO

7. POTOMAC EAGLE TRAIN

Description: Three-hour narrated train rides from Wappocomo Station, 1 mile north of Romney, wind through exceptional scenery along the South Branch Valley Railroad that includes "the trough," a narrow mountain valley. This train is a pleasant way to enjoy our national symbol, the bald eagle. The train operates from the end of May to the end of October. Call for details.

Viewing Information: This is one of the best and most dependable places to see bald eagles in the state. Eagle viewing takes place from the train. Bald eagles are present year-round, while nesting eagles can be seen from the train in May and June.

Directions: *At the intersection of U.S. Highway 50 and West Virginia State Route 28 in Romney, travel north on WV 28 for 1.4 miles to the Potomac Eagle Train. The station is on the left.*

Ownership: Potomac Eagle Scenic Railroad (800) 223-2453 or (304) 822-7464

Size: N/A   **Closest Town**: Romney

The bald eagle attains its characteristic white head and tail plumage by age five. Though rare in West Virginia, a few pairs are known to nest along the South Branch of the Potomac River. Bald eagles are spotted occasionally during the summer along West Virginia's major rivers: Cheat, Greenbrier, Kanawha, Ohio, and Potomac. During fall, migrating bald eagles are sometimes spotted from ridgetops along the Allegheny Mountains.

BILL LEA PHOTO

33

Description: At almost 23,000 acres, this is one of the largest state-owned wildlife management areas in West Virginia. Most of the scenic landscape here is Virginia pine-oak forest with about a fifth covered in oak-hickory forest.

Viewing information: Wild turkeys are common here. The largest of West Virginia's birds, they are prized by hunters and wildlife viewers alike. Turkeys are shy and wary; look for them in more open wooded areas where they search for acorns, seeds, berries, and insects. Scan the lake for nesting ospreys. This area is excellent for songbirds. Year-round residents include Carolina chickadees, tufted titmice, and northern mockingbirds. In spring several species of warblers breed here. White-tailed deer forage along the forest edge at dawn and dusk. THIS IS A NATURAL AREA WITH FEW FACILITIES AND IT IS A PUBLIC HUNTING AREA; PLEASE CHECK WITH THE MANAGER FOR SEASONS AND AFFECTED AREAS.

Directions: *Located approximately 11 miles west of Martinsburg. Near Inwood, take exit 5 off Interstate 81 and travel west on West Virginia State Route 51 about 4 miles. Turn left onto WV 45 and go west about 2.5 miles. In Glengary, turn right onto County Route 7. Travel north on CR 7 to Shanghai (about 5 miles). In Shanghai, turn left onto CR 7-13 and proceed 2 miles to the wildlife management area.*

Ownership: West Virginia Division of Natural Resources (304) 822-3551

Size: 22,928 acres   **Closest Town**: Martinsburg

The wild turkey is a wildlife management success story in the Mountain State. Intensive logging reduced numbers to about 1,000 birds at the turn of the century. Today there are about 125,000, thanks to intensive wildlife management efforts by wildlife biologists and the state.

LEN RUE JR. PHOTO

9. YANKAUER NATURE PRESERVE

Description: This 107-acre preserve is located along the banks of the Potomac River and was donated to The Nature Conservancy of West Virginia in 1967 by Dr. and Mrs. Alfred Yankauer. Owned by The Nature Conservancy and managed by the Potomac Valley Audubon Society, the preserve contains several sinkholes, oak forests, glades of redcedar, and impressive bluffs overlooking the Potomac River.

Viewing Information: White-tailed deer, pileated woodpeckers, hairy woodpeckers, wild turkeys, and box turtles occur year-round. In March, great horned owls nest in the preserve's large oaks. Many species of warblers nest here, including the prairie warbler. Look for them in May and June in the cedar thickets and in open areas. Also in May and June, look for scarlet tanagers in the hardwoods. Hike the South Trail in spring and early summer for wood thrushes and yellow-billed cuckoos. Walk the Kingfisher Trail in mid-April to early May to see many species of wildflowers in bloom, including twin leaf, cut-leaf toothwort, bloodroot, and jack-in-the-pulpit.

Directions: *From the four-way stop sign at the intersection of West Virginia State Route 45 and WV 480 in Shepherdstown, drive east toward Sharpsburg, Maryland. Turn left onto Shepherd Grade Road after 0.5 mile. Travel about 1.5 miles and turn left at the "Y" onto Scrabble Road (there is a stop sign at the "Y", but no road sign). About 1.5 miles farther, when a road intersects on the left side with Scrabble Road, stay to the right. After another 0.4 mile, stay on Scrabble Road as it turns left at yet another "Y" (there is a small barn at this intersection). Drive 2 additional miles and turn right onto County Route 5-4 (Newton School Road). The Yankauer Preserve is a little less than 0.5 mile on the right. The entrance is marked by a sign at the parking area. An informational kiosk is at the entrance to the trails.*

Ownership: The Nature Conservancy, West Virginia Chapter (304) 345-4350

Size: 107 acres   **Closest Town**: Shepherdstown

Yellow-billed cuckoos nest at Yankauer Nature Preserve.
RON AUSTING PHOTO

Description: Mixed oak and Virginia pine cover the two mountain ridges and valley that comprise the 8,000-acre Short Mountain Wildlife Management Area.

Viewing Information: Excellent access throughout the thick forest includes 15 miles of foot trails and 10 miles of gravel and dirt roads. In spring and summer, many neotropical migratory warblers and other songbirds fill the woods. White-tailed deer, black bears, wild turkeys, ruffed grouse, and many species of reptiles are also present, including West Virginia's largest snake, the black rat snake. Along the North River, look for several species of amphibians. THIS IS A NATURAL AREA WITH NO FACILITIES AND A PUBLIC HUNTING AREA; PLEASE CHECK WITH THE MANAGER FOR SEASONS AND AFFECTED AREAS.

Directions: *At the junction of U.S. Highway 50 and County Route 7 in Augusta, travel south on CR 7 (Augusta-Rio Road) for 7 miles. Turn left onto Park Road 801 at the faded Short Mountain sign. Across CR 7 from Park Road 801 is CR 7-9 (Cupps Hollow Road). Follow the dirt/gravel PR 801 0.7 mile to the wildlife management entrance.*

Ownership: West Virginia Division of Natural Resources (304) 822-3551

Size: 8,005 acres   **Closest Town**: Augusta

At more than six feet in length, the black rat snake is West Virginia's largest snake. Black rat snakes feed on rats, mice, and birds and their eggs.
LEONARD LEE RUE III PHOTO

11. SPRING RUN TROUT HATCHERY

Description: One of West Virginia's seven state-owned trout hatcheries, Spring Run offers two excellent types of viewing opportunities. The first is the remarkable number of trout that crowd the outside pools, called raceways. The second is the scenic and well-maintained Wild Trout Trail, a 100-yard nature trail that provides a glimpse into the beauty and diversity of a typical trout stream of the West Virginia highlands.

Viewing Information: First-time visitors are awed at the thousands of trout darting about the raceways. West Virginia hatcheries produce three species of trout—brook, brown, and rainbow—however, only rainbow trout are raised at Spring Run. The stunning golden-hued fish in the raceways are golden rainbow trout, a color mutation of the rainbow. Don't forget to look up, though; belted kingfishers are usually seen on the wires over the hatchery waiting for a free meal. Be sure to stroll the Wild Trout Trail. The trout in the stream along this nature trail are spooked easily; stop and stand very still to catch a glimpse of rainbow trout. Look for mink along the stream banks. Though generally nocturnal they can occasionally be seen during the day, especially in winter. Bald and golden eagles have been seen soaring above the rock cliffs .

Directions: *South of Petersburg, turn left off U.S. Highway 220 onto County Route 9 (South Mill Creek Road) and travel south on CR 9 for 4 miles to Dorcas. In Dorcas, turn left onto CR 9-2 (Spring Run Road) and proceed for 2 miles to the hatchery, on the right.*

Ownership: West Virginia Division of Natural Resources (304) 257-4188

Size: 8 acres   **Closest Town**: Petersburg

The West Virginia Centennial Golden Trout is a symbol of the state's first 100 years because its first wide-scale stocking took place in 1963, West Virginia's Centennial. Developed in state hatcheries, it is a color mutation of the rainbow trout.

DON PHARES PHOTO

12. SPRUCE KNOB AND SPRUCE KNOB LAKE

Description: At 4,861 feet, Spruce Knob is the highest mountain in the Mountain State. Its elevation, cool climate, and spruce forest give it the look and feel of a Canadian forest. Spruce Knob Lake is a beautiful 25-acre lake 9 miles west of Spruce Knob, a National Recreation Area.

Viewing Information: White-tailed deer are common; look in forest openings in the early morning or evening throughout the year. Wild turkeys, snowshoe hares, Appalachian cottontails, and northern flying squirrels are also present. Canada geese can be seen at Spruce Knob Lake between March and June. Great blue herons are present from March to July. Several species of warblers nest here, including magnolia, black-throated blue, Blackburnian, and chestnut-sided warbler. Red squirrels are common; listen for their scolding chatter. Look for bluegills and trout in the lake throughout the warmer months. THIS IS A PUBLIC HUNTING AREA; PLEASE CHECK WITH THE MANAGER FOR SEASONS AND AFFECTED AREAS.

Directions: To Spruce Knob Lake from Harman, take U.S. Highway 33 west to County Route 29 (Whitmer Road) and turn left. Travel south on CR 29 for 8.3 miles to Whitmer. Continue south on Whitmer Road for another 10.3 miles and turn left on Forest Road 1. Proceed southeast for 2.5 miles to Spruce Knob Lake. To get to Spruce Knob from Spruce Knob Lake, continue southeast on FR 1 for 0.5 mile. Turn left on FR 112, and proceed for 9 miles. Turn left on FR 104, and go 2 miles to Spruce Knob observation platform and Whispering Spruce Nature Trail.

Ownership: USDA Forest Service (304) 257-4488

Size: 25 acres   **Closest Town**: Whitmer

The snowshoe hare's white winter pelage helps camouflage it from predators in winter.

LEONARD LEE RUE III PHOTO

38

13. WATOGA STATE PARK

Description: Sheltered on three sides by the Monongahela National Forest and the Calvin Price State Forest, Watoga was the first, and is the largest state park in West Virginia. This 10,100-acre park derives its name from the Cherokee word *watauga*, which means "river of islands," because of the numerous islands and sandbars in this wide, shallow stretch of the Greenbrier River.

Viewing Information: In summer, many excellent interpretive programs orient visitors to the nature of Watoga. Beavers are sometimes seen during late evening in the lake area in spring, summer, and fall. Look for beaver dams, which consist of large piles of sticks, twigs, mud, and even small logs across streams, or large conical mounds of sticks and mud at the water's edge. Beavers are easily distinguished from West Virginia's other semiaquatic mammals—muskrat, mink, and river otter—because of their large size (adults weigh between 30 and 60 pounds) and their flat, paddle-shaped tails. Wild turkeys are abundant here in the woods along the river to your right as you enter the park. White-tailed deer also are abundant; watch for them in the early morning or late evening in forest clearings. In spring listen for the drumming of the male ruffed grouse, as its wings rapidly beat the air. Chiefly a ground and understory bird, ruffed grouse grow "snowshoes" in the winter, rows of bristles on their toes that help them get around in the deep snows that blanket this area. This is one of the few areas where the mountain earth snake occurs.

Directions: *From Hillsboro take U.S. Highway 219 for 0.9 mile, then turn right onto County Route 27. Follow CR 27 for 2.3 miles to the park entrance.*

Ownership: West Virginia Division of Natural Resources (304) 799-4087

Size: 10,100 acres   **Closest Town**: Hillsboro

This beaver is carrying mud and sticks to coat its lodge for winter.
LEN RUE JR. PHOTO

Description: Cranberry Glades is one of the most unique areas in West Virginia. Life in its four bogs, or acidic wetlands, resembles life more characteristic of the northern United States and Canada than the Appalachians, and for several of the species found in the glades, it is their southernmost range. The 750-acre botanical area, part of the Monongahela National Forest, is home to dozens of interesting species of plants, including orchids and carnivorous plants, such as the sundew. The bog forest here is composed of red spruce, hemlock, and yellow birch.

Viewing Information: Bog ground is spongy peat, partially decayed plant material, covered by sphagnum moss. Please stay on the trail and boardwalks to protect this delicate ecosystem. Start your visit by strolling the boardwalk trail. White-tailed deer are present year-round. Cranberry Glades is the southernmost breeding range for many typically northern breeding species like the purple finch and the northern waterthrush. Scan the water's edge for the waterthrush. April to July is excellent for viewing other breeding birds as well. Black bears have been seen in the skunk cabbage along the boardwalk. Hike the 6-mile Cow Pasture Trail to observe the extensive beaver ponds and alder thickets. Beavers are usually not active during the day, so the best chances of seeing, or more likely hearing one is in the evening.

Directions: From Marlinton, travel south on U.S. Highway 219. At Mill Point, turn right onto West Virginia State Route 55 and travel west on WV 55 for 6.4 miles to Cranberry Mountain Visitors Center on the left. Continue west on WV 55 for 0.6 mile, then turn right onto Forest Road 102 and travel 1.4 miles to the botanical area parking.

Ownership: USDA Forest Service, Monongahela National Forest; contact Gauley Ranger District (304) 846-2695, or Cranberry Mountain Nature Center (304) 653-4826

Size: 750 acres   **Closest Town**: Marlinton

A boardwalk through Cranberry Glades gets visitors close to the wetland without doing it harm.
STEPHEN J. SHALUTA JR. PHOTO

15. HIGHLAND SCENIC HIGHWAY

Description: Designated a National Forest Scenic Byway in 1989, this 45-mile drive leads wildlife viewers from Richwood to U.S. Highway 219, 7 miles north of Marlinton. A paved two-lane auto tour winds through the Monongahela National Forest's mountainous terrain, reaching elevations in excess of 4,500 feet. Here you'll find some of the state's most scenic regions and more than 150 miles of hiking trails can be accessed from the byway, including three barrier-free trails (Falls of Hills Creek, Cranberry Glades, and the Big Spruce Overlook).

Viewing information: In the Monongahela National Forest, which includes the 35,864-acre Cranberry Wilderness, there are 230 species of birds (159 are breeders and 71 are migratory), 72 species of fish, and more then 50 species of mammals. The forest is home to nine federally listed endangered or threatened animal and plant species. From a vehicle, visitors often see white-tailed deer, wild turkeys, hawks, ravens, gray and fox squirrels, and woodchucks, the largest member of the squirrel family in West Virginia. Hikers are rewarded with sightings of songbirds as well as red and gray foxes, snowshoe hares, raccoons, beavers, minks, opossums, ruffed grouse, and woodcocks. Occasionally, black bears and bobcats are seen. Golden eagles are rare in West Virginia, but have been seen during migration along this portion of West Virginia State Route 150. THE PARKWAY IS NOT MAINTAINED FOR WINTER TRAVEL; USE EXTREME CAUTION WHILE DRIVING. THIS IS A PUBLIC HUNTING AREA; PLEASE CHECK WITH THE MANAGER FOR SEASONS AND AFFECTED AREAS.

Directions: *From Mill Point at the junction of U.S. Highway 219 and West Virginia State Route 55, travel west on WV SR 55 for 6.4 miles to the Cranberry Mountain Visitor Center which is on the left. On the right, opposite the visitor center, is WV 150, also known as Highland Scenic Highway. Drive WV 150 north for 22 miles.*

Ownership: USDA Forest Service, Monongahela National Forest; contact Gauley Ranger District, (304) 846-2695, or Cranberry Mountain Nature Center, (304) 653-4826

Size: 45 miles   **Closest town**: Richwood

The bobcat is a secretive predator, preying mostly on rabbits and rodents at dusk and dawn.

BILL LEA PHOTO

41

Description: Located within the Monongahela National Forest, Handley is one of West Virginia's most beautiful and productive wildlife management areas. Bordering the Williams River, Handley was once a privately owned sheep and cattle farm. The area consists of bottomlands, rolling hills, and scattered steep slopes composed primarily of beech, birch, and maple. Several small ponds and a 6-acre lake provide an array of wildlife habitats. Active wildlife management by the Wildlife Resources Section has increased the quality of habitat throughout Handley since its acquisition in 1959.

Viewing Information: This area is well known for its numbers of white-tailed deer, turkeys, and ruffed grouse. Up to 100 turkeys use the area during breeding season. Black bears, beavers, red and gray foxes, muskrats, raccoons, woodchucks, and eastern cottontail rabbits are present. Look for beavers along the Williams River and around Big and Little Laurel Creeks. In spring wood ducks nest along the Williams River, and in fall American woodcock can be found in the bottomlands and shrubby field borders near the river. THIS IS A PUBLIC HUNTING AREA; PLEASE CHECK WITH THE MANAGER FOR SEASONS AND AFFECTED AREAS.

Directions: *From Marlinton, travel north on U.S. Highway 219 for 3.4 miles. Turn left onto West Virginia State Route 17 and travel west on WV 17 for 4.5 miles to a fork; continue straight for 1.6 miles and bear right at next fork (there is a sign for Handley). Proceed 1 mile to the entrance.*

Ownership: West Virginia Division of Natural Resources (304) 637-0245

Size: 784 acres   **Closest Town**: Marlinton

Red foxes are skilled hunters and prey mostly on mice during winter.
LEONARD LEE RUE III PHOTO

42

17. GAUDINEER SCENIC AREA

Description: An interesting blend of cultural and natural history meet here. Gaudineer Knob, located atop 4,445-foot-high Shavers Mountain in the Cheat Mountain Range, is a 140-acre tract of virgin red spruce–northern hardwoods forest that is 250 to 300 years old. It is a remnant of the spruce forests that originally spread across the highest mountaintops in West Virginia. The preservation of this forest was the result of a surveying mistake. Failing to correct for the difference between true north and magnetic north, a surveyor omitted this tract of land, resulting in a forgotten triangular wedge of virgin forest when the surrounding areas were logged. In 1914 the area was designated as a scenic area by the USDA Forest Service. The knob was named for Monongahela National Forest district ranger Don Gaudineer, who lost his life while trying to rescue his children from a fire in 1936.

Viewing information: The nine most common breeding birds here are magnolia warblers, solitary vireos, black-throated blue warblers, Blackburnian warblers, winter wrens, golden-crowned kinglets, black-capped chickadees, dark-eyed juncos, and chestnut-sided warblers. Early mornings and evenings from mid-May to mid-July are best to see these birds. Twenty-two species of warblers are known to summer here, more than at any other mountain in the Appalachians. Gaudineer is also an exceptional place for bird watchers to find four species of brown-backed thrushes, all premier singers, between late May and early July: hermit, Swainson's, wood thrush, and veery. In the 1940s, studies by the U.S. Fish and Wildlife Service showed that this area had one of the highest populations of birds per acre in the United States. Be sure to go to the picnic area, located 1 mile south of the scenic area, and hike the short trail to Gaudineer overlook for a spectacular view.

Directions: *From the intersection of U.S. Highway 250/92 and US 219 in Huttonsville, travel south on US 250/92 for 12.6 miles. Turn left onto Forest Road 27. Travel north on FR 27 for 2.5 miles. The parking area is on the right.*

Ownership: USDA Forest Service, Monongahela National Forest (304) 456-3335

Size: 140 acres   **Closest Town**: Durbin

Gaudineer Scenic Area lies within the Monongahela National Forest. This National Forest covers almost a million acres of the Potomac Highlands region.

Male parula warbler. RON AUSTING PHOTO

REGION TWO: NEW RIVER VALLEY/ GREENBRIER VALLEY/METRO VALLEY

Bordered by rugged mountains on the east and south, the heartland of the Mountain State on the north, and the Ohio River on the west, this region contains a wide range of wildlife habitats and viewing opportunities, from remote wild areas such as Panther State Forest to easily accessed sites such as Kanawha State Forest, only 7 miles south of Charleston. Here runs the New River, the second-oldest river in the world.

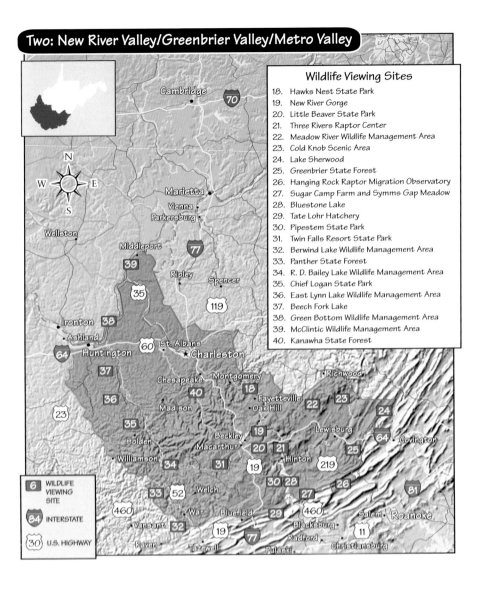

Two: New River Valley/Greenbrier Valley/Metro Valley

Wildlife Viewing Sites

18. Hawks Nest State Park
19. New River Gorge
20. Little Beaver State Park
21. Three Rivers Raptor Center
22. Meadow River Wildlife Management Area
23. Cold Knob Scenic Area
24. Lake Sherwood
25. Greenbrier State Forest
26. Hanging Rock Raptor Migration Observatory
27. Sugar Camp Farm and Symms Gap Meadow
28. Bluestone Lake
29. Tate Lohr Hatchery
30. Pipestem State Park
31. Twin Falls Resort State Park
32. Berwind Lake Wildlife Management Area
33. Panther State Forest
34. R. D. Bailey Lake Wildlife Management Area
35. Chief Logan State Park
36. East Lynn Lake Wildlife Management Area
37. Beech Fork Lake
38. Green Bottom Wildlife Management Area
39. McClintic Wildlife Management Area
40. Kanawha State Forest

6 WILDLIFE VIEWING SITE

84 INTERSTATE

30 U.S. HIGHWAY

18. HAWKS NEST STATE PARK

Description: This impressive state park offers commanding views of the New River Gorge and Hawks Nest Lake in addition to numerous wildlife. The area is typified by the river floodplain and oak-hickory forests are surrounded by high rock cliffs.

Viewing Information: Start at the Hawks Nest Overlook to look for, appropriately, hawks. Red-tailed hawks can often be seen in summer during the warmer parts of the day as they catch a free ride along the wind currents over the canyon. Make your way to the lake and river to look for common loons, which can be spotted during migration in spring and fall. Search here for great blue herons and belted kingfishers, which can often be seen perched near or hovering above the water, ready to seize an unwary fish. Kingfishers are easily identified by their big head, big bill, and head crest. Females have brown breastbands; males do not. Throughout the park in summer, look for eastern bluebirds, Baltimore orioles, and scarlet tanagers. On sunny days you might see one of the park's many species of reptiles: black rat snakes, northern fence lizards, or five-lined and broadhead skinks.

Directions: *From the junction of U.S. Highway 19 and US 60, travel west on US 60 for 7.7 miles to the park entrance. The park is on the south side of US 60.*

Ownership: West Virginia Division of Natural Resources (304) 658-5212

Size: 276 acres   **Closest Town:** Ansted

Male bluebirds like this one are brighter and more colorful than females. Bluebirds nest in cavities in trees and old fence posts.
RON AUSTING PHOTO

19. NEW RIVER GORGE

Description: Visitors are impressed by the spectacular views of the New River Gorge. The New River area, managed by the National Park Service, is composed of a collection of federal, state, and private lands surrounding this national river. Babcock State Park lies within the area; however, much of the land is still private, so please respect the owners' rights while watching wildlife. The Canyon Rim Visitor Center on U.S. Highway 19 on the north side of the river affords fabulous views of the gorge as well as the US 19 bridge. This 3,030-foot-long bridge rises 876 feet above the river and is the world's largest single steel arch bridge. Acclaimed for its wildlife viewing opportunities, the river is known for its whitewater rafting, considered to be some of the best in the East. The New River is not new in geologic terms—it is the second oldest river in the world after the Nile River in Egypt.

Viewing Information: White-tailed deer are usually seen in forest openings throughout the area. Black bears, bobcats, beavers, opossums, raccoons, and several species of bats are present, though most are nocturnal. Four male and two female river otters were released in the New River by the Wildlife Resources Section in 1996. Two species of fox, red and gray, inhabit the park. Red foxes prefer more open areas, whereas gray foxes tend to prefer more wooded areas, especially those in early successional stages. Both species feed primarily on cottontails and rodents. In the woodlands during the day, search for wild turkeys and ruffed grouse, and at night listen for owls—barred, great horned, and eastern screech. A population of river cooters—large turtles—inhabits the New River. West Virginia's largest skink, the broadhead, occurs in the gorge. Many aquatic animals inhabit the river, including smallmouth bass, rock bass, redbreast sunfish, logperch, common carp, muskellunge, whitetail shiners, channel catfish, freshwater sponges, and mussels.

Directions: *The Canyon Rim Visitor Center is located immediately east of where U.S. Highway 19 crosses the New River Gorge, just north of Fayetteville.*

Ownership: National Park Service (304) 465-0508

Size: 70,000 acres   **Closest Town:** Fayetteville

New River
Gorge
National
River.
JIM CLARK PHOTO

Description: Eighteen-acre Little Beaver Lake is nestled in rolling mountains of pine and hardwood just west of Beckley. This small park's easy access, excellent trails, and beautiful scenery make it an excellent day trip for watching wildlife.

Viewing Information: Summer months are best. White-tailed deer can be seen throughout. Hike the Railroad Grade Trail into the heart of the park to see turkeys, and listen for the many resident bird species. Many of the park's mammals, such as black bears, raccoons, opossums, minks, beavers, and bobcats, are more active in the evening. Mallards and Canada geese can usually be seen around the lake.

Directions: *East of Beckley, take Exit 129A off Interstate 64. Travel south for 2 miles and turn left at the sign to enter the park.*

Ownership: West Virginia Division of Natural Resources (304) 763-2494

Size: 562 acres   **Closest Town:** Beckley

Mink, semiaquatic mammals, are secretive and nocturnal and seeing them is a challenge for wildlife viewers. JOHN GERLACH PHOTO

21. THREE RIVERS AVIAN CENTER

Description: Perched on a 102-acre wildlife sanctuary high above the New River Gorge National River, this privately owned center provides veterinary and rehabilitative care to injured, displaced, and orphaned birds of prey, as well as herons. The center boasts an annual release rate above the national average.

Viewing Information: Several species of raptors are kept at the center for educational purposes, including a great horned owl, barn owl, common screech owl, barred owl, American kestrel, red-tailed hawk, and broad-winged hawk. Educational programs emphasizing public involvement in ecosystem stewardship and natural resource conservation are offered. Scheduled on-site tours are available. Public tours are on the first Saturday of each month, May through October from 1 P.M. to 5 P.M. BROOKS MOUNTAIN ROAD IS STEEP AND UNPAVED.

Directions: *From Interstate 64, take the Sandstone exit 139. Travel south on West Virginia State Route 20 toward Hinton for 5.8 miles. Turn left onto Brooks Mountain Road and follow the signs for 2.7 miles to Three Rivers Avian Center.*

Ownership: Three Rivers Avian Center (800) 721-5252 (in West Virginia), or (304) 466-4683

Size: 102 acres   **Closest Town:** Hinton

Identify a great horned owl by its large size, ear tufts (or "horns") and white throat collar. Note its yellow eyes compared to the barred owl's brown eyes.

JIM ROETZEL PHOTO

Description: At Meadow River, hike or walk near the wetlands along the river of this natural and undeveloped area.

Viewing Information: The wetlands here provide some of the best viewing in this management area. In spring and summer look for wood ducks, one of our most beautiful ducks. Males, or drakes, are more colorful than females (hens). During spring and fall migration, many species of waterfowl such as mallards and blue- and green-winged teals use these wetlands to rest. During spring, listen for some common frogs of West Virginia: northern spring peepers (a clear, single high-pitched note or "*peep*"), bullfrogs ("*jug-o'-rum*"), pickerel frogs (a low-pitched "snore"), and green frogs ("*c'tung*"). Great blue herons use the marsh; look for them in the shallows waiting for a fish or a frog. From 1992 to 1996, river otters were released in the Meadow River by the Wildlife Resources Section. Otters feed between early and midmorning and then again in the evening. THIS IS A NATURAL AREA WITH NO FACILITIES AND A PUBLIC HUNTING AREA; PLEASE CHECK WITH THE MANAGER FOR SEASONS AND AFFECTED AREAS.

Directions: *Take Sam Black Church Exit 156 off Interstate 64 to travel west on U.S. Highway 60 for 5 miles. Turn left onto County Route 60-18 (Tommy Hall Road), and proceed to the wildlife management area (left of the road). Park along Tommy Hall Road for access to the area. Tommy Hall Road is 1.3 miles long and dead-ends into private property.*

Ownership: West Virginia Division of Natural Resources (304) 256-6947; West Virginia Division of Highways (304) 558-3505.

Size: 2,495 acres   **Closest Town:** Rupert

Reaching lengths of 6 to 7 inches, the bullfrog is West Virginia's largest frog.
JIM CLARK PHOTO

23. COLD KNOB SCENIC AREA

Description: Owned by Westvaco Corporation, this is an impressive and imposing mountain in a state known for its mountains. At 4,200 feet, Cold Knob is characterized by large rock outcrops and formations and sweeping vistas of the Allegheny Mountains and Greenbrier Valley. It is a mixed area with open, grassy meadows and thick northern hardwood forests at the summit.

Viewing Information: Cold Knob is located on the Allegheny Front, an important migration corridor for many birds of prey, and is one of the best places for viewing these birds during fall migration. In September and October, patient wildlife viewers may view migrating ospreys, bald eagles, golden eagles, northern harriers, and northern goshawks as they make their way from the northeastern United States and eastern Canada to southern wintering grounds. Cold fronts often "push" migrating birds south in the fall. Watch for cold fronts—the bigger the better—coming down from Canada in September, and time your trip to Cold Knob accordingly. Look for Cooper's hawks, American kestrels, sharp-shinned hawks, and red-shouldered hawks year-round . White-tailed deer and black bears are also present here. THIS IS A NATURAL AREA WITH NO FACILITIES. USE CAUTION ON THE UNPAVED ROAD TO COLD KNOB. SOME AREAS ARE OPEN TO HUNTING; PLEASE CHECK WITH THE MANAGER FOR SEASONS AND AFFECTED AREAS.

Directions: *At Lewisburg, take Exit 169 off Interstate 64 onto U.S. Highway 219. Travel north for 8.7 miles to Frankford. Turn left onto County Route 17 (Williamsburg Road) and go west for 8.4 miles to Williamsburg. Turn right onto CR 9 and travel north for 3.2 miles. Then left onto CR 10 (Trout Road) and travel north for 5.9 miles. At the sign for the scenic area turn right; the parking area is 0.1 mile past the sign.*

Ownership: Westvaco Corporation (304) 392-6373

Size: 32 acres   **Closest Town:** Frankford

A raptor characterized by grace and strength, the Northern goshawk can be identified by the white stripe over the eye.
RON AUSTING PHOTO

NEW RIVER VALLEY

Description: Lake Sherwood, a 165-acre impoundment, is the largest lake in the Monongahela National Forest. Eight trails cross the area and lead hikers and wildlife watchers around the lake and up nearby mountains through a variety of habitats and offer sweeping views of the countryside.

Viewing Information: White-tailed deer are best seen during spring and fall along any of Lake Sherwood's trails. Waterfowl are often present in spring and fall on Lake Sherwood. Ruffed grouse and wild turkeys inhabit the forested areas away from the lake. Because this is a popular recreational spot, seek out the quieter areas to view these species. Beavers, primarily a nocturnal species, are present. Great blue herons are present during cooler months, and green herons summer here. Search for three species of owls (barred, eastern screech, and great horned) by looking for owl pellets (undigested remains of prey in coughed up pellet form) under pine trees. Four species of squirrels can be seen: gray, red, fox, and the nocturnal southern flying.

Directions: *At the intersection of West Virginia State Route 92 and WV 14 in Neola, travel east on WV 14 (Lake Sherwood Road) for 11 miles to the recreation area.*

Ownership: USDA Forest Service (304) 536-2144

Size: 165 acres   **Closest Town:** Neola

Barred owls are usually seen before they are heard. Listen for their characteristic, loud, high-pitched hooting at night and on overcast days.
BILL LEA PHOTO

25. GREENBRIER STATE FOREST

Description: Easy access from Interstate 64 coupled with heavily forested mountain terrain make this 5,100-acre state forest an ideal place for wildlife viewing day trips. Nine well-maintained trails accommodate levels of hiking ability from easy to difficult and offer the viewer a range of habitat: old fields, logging roads, and sweeping mountaintop vistas from atop Kates Mountain.

Viewing Information: Nestor's Field Forest Management Road is a good place to see white-tailed deer in the early morning and evening. Wildlife watching is especially good along the forest edge. An edge is where two habitats meet, in this case an old field and the forest. Deer, wild turkeys, and many other species of birds can feed in the field but be close enough to the forest where they can take cover should danger appear. On summer nights, listen for the whip-poor-will, calling its name over and over. You won't hear this bird in the winter, though. The whip-poor-will winters throughout the Gulf states down to Honduras. SOME AREAS ARE OPEN TO HUNTING; PLEASE CHECK WITH THE MANAGER FOR SEASONS AND AFFECTED AREAS.

Directions: *From Interstate 64, take exit 175 and travel south on County Route 60-14. Follow the signs to Greenbrier State Forest, about 1 mile from the interstate. As you enter the forest, stop for information at the forest office, which will be on your left. Less than 2 miles past the entrance will be the picnic area, again on the left.*

Ownership: West Virginia Division of Natural Resources (304) 536-1944

Size: 5,100 acres   **Closest Town:** White Sulphur Springs

NEW RIVER VALLEY

Whip-poor-will. RON AUSTING PHOTO

26. HANGING ROCK RAPTOR MIGRATION OBSERVATORY

Description: Geography, geology, and wind currents make Hanging Rock one of the premier places in West Virginia to observe migrating birds of prey in the fall. The observatory is located on the westernmost ridge of the Ridge and Valley Province, where conditions are ideal for a major flight path southward. Prevailing westerly winds rising over the Peters Mountain escarpment create a long glide path for these birds and an ideal place to view them. As a bonus, hawk watchers are treated to sweeping 360-degree views of the parallel ridges of the Ridge and Valley Province to the south and the Allegheny Plateau to the north. The observatory has been used by the Brooks Bird Club to research fall raptor migration for the past 30 years. A reconstructed fire tower serves as an observation platform.

Viewing Information: Hike one mile to the observatory between late August and late October to view numerous migrating species: broad-winged, Cooper's, sharp-shinned, red-shouldered, and rough-legged hawks, American kestrels, bald eagles, golden eagles, ospreys, and peregrine falcons. THIS IS A NATURAL AREA WITH NO FACILITIES.

Directions: At Rock Camp, turn off U.S. Highway 219 onto County Route 29 (Zenith Road) and travel 10.4 miles to CR 15 (Waiteville Road). Proceed south for 1.7 miles to the top of the mountain; park on the right. Hike the Allegheny Trail west along the ridgeline for 0.8 mile to the junction with the blue-blazed trail on the left that leads to the observation platform in 0.1 mile.

Ownership: USDA Forest Service (540) 552-4641

Size: N/A.   **Closest Town:** Waiteville

Autumn is the best time to see Cooper's hawks as they migrate through West Virginia to points south for the winter.
LEN RUE JR. PHOTO

54

27. SUGAR CAMP FARM AND SYMMS GAP MEADOW

Description: These sites lie adjacent to the Appalachian Trail. An 8-mile round-trip hike is required to reach Symms Gap Meadow, a large cleared area that offers sweeping vistas.

Viewing Information: Begin this hike from the parking area on the blue-blazed Groundhog Trail through Sugar Camp Farm to the top of Peters Mountain and the Appalachian Trail (2 miles). Turn right (southwest) on the Appalachian Trail and hike 2 miles to Symms Gap Meadow (Will's Field).White-tailed deer are abundant year-round. Look for wild turkeys from April to June. Will's Field is an excellent place to view migrating hawks in September and October, and black bears have also been spotted in this field. Both Sugar Camp and Will's Field are good places to see butterflies. On warm, dry mornings along field edges, look for male Diana butterflies in late June and July, and for females in July and August. They're easy to tell apart: the outer third of the male's wings is bright orange; the lower inner wing of the female is a pale blue and the upper wing has white spots on black. THESE ARE NATURAL AREAS WITH NO FACILITIES.

Directions: *At the intersection of U.S. Highway 460 and US 219 in Rich Creek, Virginia, travel north on US 219 to Peterstown, West Virginia. Continue north through Peterstown for 6 miles to County Route 219-21 (Painter Run Road). Turn right onto Painter Run Road and follow it for 1.8 miles to the fenced parking spot on the right.*

Ownership: USDA Forest Service (540) 552-4641

Size: Sugar Camp Farm, 140 acres; Will's Field, 15 acres

Closest Town: Peterstown

The sex of a Diana butterfly is easily identified. The male is bright orange and brown and the female is black with white spots and pale blue on the hindwing.
RICHARD CECH PHOTOS

28. BLUESTONE LAKE WILDLIFE MANAGEMENT AREA

Description: Bluestone Lake was formed with the completion of Bluestone Dam in 1949. The area surrounding the 2,000-acre lake is a complex of federal and state lands. Begin your wildlife viewing trip at Bluestone State Park, but be sure to visit the dam and surrounding lands.

Viewing Information: Miles of shoreline and acres of open water attract a variety of waterfowl; mallards and Canada geese are present year-round. From December to April look for common goldeneyes, buffleheads, and hooded mergansers in the spillway below the dam. In March and April search for ring-necked ducks and lesser scaups above Bluestone Dam, and in summer look for wood ducks along islands in the river. Bald eagles are present year-round but are more common in winter; search around the lake and below Hinton. Great blue herons are year-round residents, and green herons can be viewed during the summer. SOME AREAS ARE OPEN TO HUNTING; PLEASE CHECK WITH THE MANAGER FOR SEASONS AND AFFECTED AREAS.

Directions: From Interstate 64, take the Sandstone exit 139. Travel south on West Virginia State Route 20 for 16 miles.

Ownership: U.S. Army Corp of Engineers (304) 466-0156 or (304) 466-1234; West Virginia Division of Natural Resources (304) 466-2805

Size: 2,040 acres   **Closest Town:** Hinton

29. TATE LOHR HATCHERY

Description: Tate Lohr is not a hatchery, but a rearing station where trout are raised from fingerlings to stocking size in four outdoor circular pools.

Viewing Information: About 20,000 rainbow and golden rainbow trout are reared here each year. The golden rainbow trout is not a different species but a color mutation of the regular rainbow, developed at the Petersburg Hatchery through selective breeding.

Directions: From Princeton, travel east on U.S. Highway 460 for 9 miles. Take the Oakvale exit and go west on West Virginia State Route 112 for 0.1 mile. Bear left on County Route 460-6 (Kellysville Road) and after another 0.1 mile turn right (this turn could easily be missed because there is no sign and it looks like a pull-out). Follow this gravel road for 3.8 miles to the hatchery, on the left.

Ownership: West Virginia Division of Natural Resources (304) 898-3221

Size: 150 acres   **Closest Town:** Princeton

30. PIPESTEM STATE PARK

Description: Oak-hickory forests laced with grassy fields, rock outcroppings, and sweeping views of the 1,000-foot-deep Bluestone River Gorge beckon exploration at Pipestem. Named after the hollow pipestem bush that Native Americans and early settlers used for making pipes, this park offers wildlife viewers more than 17 miles of trails through and near the four major habitats of the park: open water, wetland, old field, and hardwood forest.

Viewing Information: Excellent wildlife viewing has been made even better through interpretive programs and educational materials at the nature center wildlife observation area. Approximately 161 species of birds have been recorded at the state park, and the area has one of the highest densities of wild turkeys in the state; they can be seen at several locations. Waterfowl can easily be seen between March and November on Long Branch Lake. From the lookout tower, look for turkey vultures and several species of hawks. In September broad-winged hawks migrate in large flocks, sometimes numbering several hundred. From December to April look for bald eagles from this spot, and from December to February, you might be lucky enough to see a golden eagle. Thirty species of warblers have been identified in the park, 20 of which nest here. Mammals include white-tailed deer, several species of shrews, moles, bats, squirrels, red and gray foxes, minks, bobcats, and mice. Look for woodchucks in clearings along the park road. In 1996 and 1997, two female and three male river otters were released in the Bluestone River by the Wildlife Resources Section. Several invertebrates can be seen here. In summer in the milkweeds, look for monarchs with their characteristic burnt-orange color and black veins. At night and early morning, look for dobsonflies, luna moths, polyphemous moths, and regal moths near Mountain Creek Lodge (located at the base of the canyon).

Directions: *Take Athens Exit 14 off Interstate 77, and travel east on County Route 7 to West Virginia State Route 20. Go north for 10 miles to the park entrance, on the left.*

Ownership: Division of Natural Resources (304) 466-1800

Size: 4,023 acres   **Closest Town:** Pipestem

Broad-winged hawk.
LEONARD LEE RUE III PHOTO

31. TWIN FALLS RESORT STATE PARK

Description: Oak-hickory and hemlock forests dominate this 3,776-acre park. Natural and manmade openings in the forest provide acres of edge-type habitat and numerous wildlife viewing opportunities. Nine trails traverse the park.

Viewing Information: Look for white-tailed deer along the forest edge and in and around the golf course. A variety of songbirds fill the forest, especially in spring and summer when many neotropical migrants come to the park to breed. Red-tailed hawks are common, especially during midday. Three species of owls are year-round residents: eastern screech, great horned, and barred. Wild turkeys are commonly seen during late summer and fall, and less frequently in the spring and early summer. Elusive black bears and gray foxes are sometimes seen. The rhododendron, West Virginia's state flower, is particularly impressive here.

Directions: *The park is located 24 miles from Interstate 64/77. Take Exit 42 off I-64/77 at Beckley and travel south on West Virginia State Route 16. Follow signs to the park. Travel on WV 16 for 3.7 miles, then take WV 54 south for 13.5 miles to Maben. Take WV 97 west from Maben for 5.3 miles to a T, turn left, and proceed for 0.6 mile to the park entrance.*

Ownership: West Virginia Division of Natural Resources (304) 294-4000

Size: 3,776 acres   **Closest Town:** Maben

The screech owl is a small owl measuring only 7 to 10 inches in length. This species has two color variations, red and gray.
BILL LEA PHOTO

32. BERWIND LAKE WILDLIFE MANAGEMENT AREA

Description: With abundant and diverse wildlife, rugged Appalachian hardwood forests, picturesque 20-acre Berwind Lake, and hiking trails and old logging roads for access, this management area is one of West Virginia's best kept.

Viewing Information: This is one of the best places in the state to see warblers and other neotropical migrants, especially during spring migration. The more common species are rose-breasted grosbeaks, kinglets (both species), white-eyed vireos, solitary vireos, yellow-breasted chats, and lots of warblers: black and white, worm-eating, Tennessee, northern parula, and yellow, for example. Around Berwind Lake look for white-tailed deer, wild turkeys, ruffed grouse, beavers, muskrats, black bears, fox and gray squirrels, red-spotted newts, gray tree frogs, and American toads. Along the shoreline scan for spotted sandpipers, water snakes, and box turtles. In spring inspect the shallow portions of the lake and ephemeral waters around the lake—they are breeding grounds for spring peepers and chorus frogs. In the evenings, listen for barred, great horned, and screech owls and for gray foxes during their courtship. Woodpeckers here include pileated, flicker, downy, hairy, and red-bellied and yellow-bellied sapsucker. Winter birds include evening grosbeaks, purple finches, pine siskins, and juncos. Several families of wood ducks use the lake in fall and winter, and in winter the lake is a resting spot for many waterfowl including ring-necked ducks, buffleheads, scaups, pied-billed grebes, blue-winged teals, hooded mergansers, and ruddy ducks. THIS IS A PUBLIC HUNTING AREA; PLEASE CHECK WITH THE MANAGER FOR SEASONS AND AFFECTED AREAS.

Directions: *Berwind Lake Wildlife Management Area is south of Welch. From Welch, take West Virgina State Route 16 south for 12 miles. At War, turn right onto County Route 12-4 and follow it to the wildlife management area.*

Ownership: Berwind Land Corporation; West Virginia Division of Natural Resources (304) 256-6947

Size: 18,000 acres   **Closest Town:** War

Spotted sandpipers have a distinctive flight pattern when flushed from shore: rapid wing beats followed by brief glides followed by rapid wing beats.

JIM ROETZEL PHOTO

33. PANTHER STATE FOREST

Description: This remote state forest is located in the rugged mountains of southern West Virginia. Miles of trails lead wildlife viewers well off the beaten path.

Viewing Information: Opportunities abound for viewing the spring migration of warblers and other neotropical migrants. Many species nest here, including white-eyed vireos, yellow breasted chats, red-eyed vireos, northern parula warblers, yellow warblers, hooded warblers, ovenbirds, and common yellowthroats. Five-lined skinks, northern fence lizards, common snapping turtles, and eastern box turtles are present. White-tailed deer, wild turkeys, and ruffed grouse can also be seen here. The Panther Creek area is especially good for catching a glimpse of a fish, frog, or crayfish hiding beneath a rock. THIS IS A PUBLIC HUNTING AREA; PLEASE CHECK WITH THE MANAGER FOR SEASONS AND AFFECTED AREAS.

Directions: *From West Virginia State Route 52, 1 mile north of Iaeger, turn at the forest sign to Panther. At the Panther post office, turn left at the sign and follow the road 3.5 miles to the forest entrance.*

Ownership: West Virginia Division of Natural Resources (304) 938-2252

Size: 10,640 acres   **Closest Town:** Panther

The yellow-breasted chat is identified by its white spectacles and bright yellow breast. Common yellowthroats are similar in appearance to yellow-breasted chats, and are sometimes confused with them. However, a male yellowthroat has a black mask while the female yellowthroat lacks the white spectacles of the yellow-breasted chat. RON AUSTING PHOTO

Description: Narrow valleys and steep ridges surround 630-acre R.D. Bailey Lake at this large, popular wildlife management area. The vast oak-hickory forest provides habitat for numerous wildlife species.

Viewing Information: Look for several species of warblers and other neotropical migrants in spring. Other breeding birds in the area include eastern kingbirds, cardinals, white-breasted nuthatches, tufted titmice, Carolina chickadees, eastern phoebes, eastern wood-pewees, Acadian flycatchers, song sparrows, Carolina wrens, blue jays, brown creepers, brown thrashers, catbirds, wood thrushes, robins, blue-gray gnatcatchers, cedar waxwings, red-winged blackbirds, Baltimore orioles, summer tanagers, indigo buntings, goldfinches, eastern towhees, chipping sparrows, and field sparrows. In addition to several species of amphibians and reptiles, white-tailed deer, raccoons, black bears, gray foxes, bobcats, Virginia opossums, minks, muskrats, striped skunks, and several bat species are found here. Twenty river otters were released in the Guyandotte River near Baileysville in 1996. THIS IS A PUBLIC HUNTING AREA; PLEASE CHECK WITH THE MANAGER FOR SEASONS AND AFFECTED AREAS.

Directions: *From Pineville, travel west on WV SR 97 for 20 miles. Turn right onto County Route 6-2 (Coal Mountain Long Branch Road) and proceed for 0.7 mile to Guyandotte Point Recreation Area.*

Ownership: U.S. Army Corp of Engineers (304) 664-3229; West Virginia Division of Natural Resources (304) 256-6947; R.D. Bailey Wildlife Management Area (304) 682-8633

Size: 17,280 acres   **Closest Town:** Pineville

NEW RIVER VALLEY

Raccoons are omnivores, eating everything from crayfish to fruits, berries, and seeds. Raccoons are known for "washing" their food before eating it. Biologists feel that this behavior is not related to "cleansing" food but rather "feeling" the food before it is eaten. BILL LEA PHOTO

35. CHIEF LOGAN STATE PARK

Description: Eight well-maintained trails provide access to most areas of this 3,300-acre mountainous park, composed mainly of poplar, beech, and maple forests. In spring and summer, wildflowers are abundant throughout, including the rare Guyandotte beauty, which blooms in May.

Viewing Information: Chief Logan is a popular place during the summer and on weekends, and serves as a major recreational facility to many nearby towns; seek out quieter sections of the park for wildlife viewing. Go early or stay later in the evening to see year-round residents: white-tailed deer, wild turkeys, and red-shouldered, red-tailed, and sharp-shinned hawks. Animal exhibits in seminatural habitats feature bobcats, wild boars, red-tailed and red-shouldered hawks, barred owls, black rat snakes, copperheads, and timber rattlesnakes.

Directions: From Chapmanville, travel south on U.S. Highway 119 for 5 miles. At the sign for Chief Logan State Park turn left onto Old Logan Road. The park entrance is 4.6 miles on the right.

Ownership: West Virginia Division of Natural Resources (304) 792-7125

Size: 3,300 acres   **Closest Town:** Logan

Red-tailed hawks are members of the buteo family, and are large, heavyset hawks with rounded tails. Red-tailed hawks prefer open habitats where they feed mainly on small rodents.
LEONARD LEE RUE III PHOTO

Description: Steep terrain covered in oak-hickory forest and crowned by 905-acre East Lynn Lake characterizes this management area.

Viewing Information: White-tailed deer, raccoons, ruffed grouse, and turkeys are present. The extensive oak-hickory forest here is an important source of mast for wild turkeys. Mast, a high energy food, is the backbone of the wild turkey's winter diet. Search the forest floors for wild turkeys because these large birds spend much of their time walking. In flight, these birds are impressive, flying up to 55 miles per hour. Sexes are easy to tell apart. Adult males, called toms or gobblers, weigh about 20 pounds (about twice as big as the females, called hens) and have coarse beards on their breasts. Although some hens have beards, they are not nearly as full. Intensive logging in the state almost wiped out the wild turkey and in 1900 only about 1,000 birds inhabited the state. However, due to intensive wildlife management, biologists estimate there are up to 170,000 wild turkeys inhabiting West Virginia. SOME AREAS ARE OPEN TO HUNTING; PLEASE CHECK THE WITH MANAGER FOR SEASONS AND AFFECTED AREAS.

Directions: *At the intersection of West Virginia State Route 152 and WV 37 in Wayne travel east on WV 37 for 9.1 miles to the East Lynn Lake entrance sign. WV 37 runs through the management area, offering numerous access points.*

Ownership: U.S. Army Corps of Engineers (304) 849-2355; West Virginia Division of Natural Resources (304) 849-9861

Size: 22,928 acres   **Closest Town:** Wayne

NEW RIVER VALLEY

The sex of a wild turkey is easy to distinguish. The turkey on the left is an adult male, called a tom or gobbler. Note its larger size and coarse beard. On the right is the female, or hen. Hens are smaller than males and have buff-colored tips on breast feathers, and do not have spurs on the rear of each leg, like gobblers do.

RON AUSTING PHOTO

37. BEECH FORK LAKE

Description: The Beech Fork Lake area is a complex of publicly owned lands surrounding 720-acre Beech Fork Lake that includes Beech Fork State Park, Beech Fork Lake Wildlife Management Area, Stowers Branch Beach and Picnic Area, and Bowen Day Use Area. Beech Fork Lake Wildlife Management Area is the largest at 7,531 acres while Beech Fork State Park is the second at 3,100 acres. Although open water and shoreline dominate the landscape, other habitats include old farmlands and pasturelands, wetlands, and oak-hickory-pine forests.

Viewing Information: Several species of hawks can be seen at Beech Fork year-round. In open areas and fields look for red-tailed and broad-winged hawks, and for red-shouldered hawks in the woodlands and along timbered wetlands. Barred owls are more often heard than seen. At night, listen for them in deep wooded areas, calling "Hoo, hoo, hoo, hoo. Hoo, hoo-hooo-aw." The "aw" at the end is a trademark, and if you hear it, you can be sure it's a barred owl. Seeing barred owls is more difficult; search thick groves of trees in the low, wet forests. In spring, look for wood ducks in small secluded ponds and wetlands around the lake, and in May search the open waters and shallows of the lake for blue-winged teals. April to early May is an excellent time to see ospreys near feeder streams and headwaters. Several species of wading birds show up at Beech Fork Lake. From August to April, great blue herons are present around the shoreline and along feeder streams; green herons are best sighted between April and October, and great egrets pass through in early May. Between July and September, numerous butterflies are present, including swallowtails, monarchs, and skippers. Amphibians are abundant: spring peepers, American toads, Fowler's toads, gray tree frogs, mountain chorus frogs, wood frogs, pickerel frogs, and West Virginia's largest frogs, bullfrogs. Turtles include eastern box, eastern spiny softshell, and snapping. Snakes are also abundant and include eastern garter, ringneck, eastern hognose, eastern milk, eastern king, black rat, northern red-bellied, northern water, and the smooth green, which is at the southernmost portion of its range. Timber rattlesnakes and copperheads are present but seldom seen. Mammals include white-tailed deer, gray and red foxes, cottontail rabbits, raccoons, skunks, and flying squirrels. An occasional bobcat has been spotted drinking along the shoreline near the campground. SOME AREAS HERE ARE PUBLIC HUNTING AREAS; PLEASE CHECK WITH THE MANAGER FOR SEASONS AND AFFECTED AREAS.

Directions: *From Interstate 64, take Exit 8 onto West Virginia State Route 152 south and proceed for 5.3 miles. In Lavalette, at the sign for Beech Fork Lake, turn left onto County Route 13, and go east for 2.2 miles to the marina entrance. If you are headed to the campground, from 64, take Exit 11 onto WV 10. Turn right onto Hughes Branch Road and follow this road to the park entrance.*

Ownership: U.S. Army Corp of Engineers (304) 522-0350 or (304) 525-4831; West Virginia Division of Natural Resources (304) 522-0303

Size: 720 acres   **Closest Town:** Lavalette

38. GREEN BOTTOM WILDLIFE MANAGEMENT AREA

Description: Stretching along the banks of the Ohio River, this management area is a network of agricultural lands, forestlands, wetlands, and open water. Bottomland hardwoods dominate the areas along the stream's bank, whereas oak and hickory dominate the steeper portions of the area.

Viewing Information: The various habitats at Green Bottom support a diversity of wildlife that includes 30 species of mammals, 105 species of birds in the fall and 47 species in the winter, 12 species of amphibians, and 5 species of reptiles. In early spring, bald eagles migrate through. Canada geese can be seen nesting throughout the wetlands and on any of the 14 manmade nesting islands at Green Bottom Swamp. Wood ducks nest in natural cavities and in any of the 50 nesting boxes constructed by the Wildlife Resources Section. Gray and red foxes live here. Red foxes prefer more open habitat and are seldom found in dense woodlands; gray foxes can be found in open habitats but seem to prefer forests in the early successional stages of development. Other mammals include minks, muskrats, raccoons, white-tailed deer, and beavers. Amphibians in the area include leopard frog and Jefferson salamander. Early August is particularly beautiful at Green Bottom when marsh roses cover the wetlands. THIS IS A PUBLIC HUNTING AREA; PLEASE CHECK WITH THE MANAGER FOR SEASONS AND AFFECTED AREAS.

Directions: *From Huntington, travel north on West Virginia State Route 2 for 16 miles. There are several access points to the area on the west side of WV 2 just south of the Cabell and Mason county line.*

Ownership: U.S. Army Corp of Engineers; West Virginia Division of Natural Resources (304) 675-0871

Size: 1,100 acres   **Closest Town:** Glenwood

The male wood duck is one of the more beautiful ducks to grace West Virginia's waters.

LEN RUE JR. PHOTO

39. McCLINTIC WILDLIFE MANAGEMENT AREA

Description: One of the wildlife viewing treasures in this region, this diverse wildlife management area boasts numerous habitat types including wetlands, mixed hardwood forests, farmlands, and brushlands. Active wildlife management efforts by the Wildlife Resources Section such as the planting of hedges, seeding, and the construction of ponds have increased the productivity of this area since its acquisition in 1950.

Viewing Information: Each habitat at McClintic offers different wildlife viewing opportunities. Nineteen of the management area's 39 ponds are managed for waterfowl and aquatic furbearers, such as minks and beavers. They are nocturnal, so search for them shortly after sundown. Waterfowl viewing is excellent here for Canada geese, wood ducks, mallards, black ducks, gadwalls, and blue- and green-winged teals. In the forests look for white-tailed deer, wild turkeys, gray and fox squirrels, and ruffed grouse. Bobwhites prefer farmlands and pastures. Bobwhites are usually heard before they're seen; listen for their trademark, "*bob WHITE, bob WHITE.*" This management area is located in Mason County, the only known range in West Virginia of the midland smooth softshell, which occurs in rivers, creeks, ponds, and lakes. THIS IS A NATURAL AREA WITH FEW FACILITIES, AND IT IS A PUBLIC HUNTING AREA; PLEASE CHECK WITH THE MANAGER FOR SEASONS AND AFFECTED AREAS.

Directions: *At the intersection of West Virginia State Route 2 and WV 62 in Point Pleasant, travel north on WV 62 for 6.4 miles. Turn right at the management area sign and travel east for 1.6 miles. The wildlife management area will be on your left.*

Ownership: West Virginia Division of Natural Resources (304) 675-0871

Size: 2,788 acres   **Closest Town:** Point Pleasant

The sex of a bobwhite is easily identified. The throat and the eyebrow are white, as on the male pictured here. On the female, they are buff.
BILL LEA PHOTO

40. KANAWHA STATE FOREST

Description: Kanawha State Forest is a favorite for many Charleston residents. Because the forest is only 7 miles south of the city, it is also popular with people throughout West Virginia and the entire East Coast, who are fascinated by the state's wildflowers, amphibian life, and birds.

Viewing Information: Nineteen hiking trails in the forest provide access to many excellent wildlife viewing sites. Mammals here include white-tailed deer, bobcats; red and gray foxes; raccoons; red, gray, and fox squirrels; southern flying squirrels; white-footed mice; and black bears. Nineteen species of wood warblers are here in summer along with dozens of other species. It has been reported that there are more birds at Kanawha than anywhere else in the state. The Spotted Salamander Trail provides some of the most accessible and best amphibian viewing in the state. The wetland at this site is a vernal pool that dries out between June and October. The best time to view amphibians here is spring. From February to April, with the first warm rains, spotted salamanders leave their burrows and migrate to breeding sites at night. They are easily identified by their bright yellow spots. Also at this time, watch for small, brown, four-toed salamanders. Though marbled salamanders breed in October, their larvae are present and transform in April or May. Other amphibians that might be heard or seen along this trail include green frogs, calling in April and May, wood frogs, calling and breeding from February to April, spring peepers, calling and breeding from March to May, American toads calling in May and June, Fowler's toads, calling throughout the summer, mountain chorus frogs calling and breeding in April and May, and gray tree frogs, calling and breeding in May and June. Several of the forest's trails (Beech Glen, Balanced Rock, and Mary Draper Ingles) pass by massive sandstone overhangs that harbor woodrat middens. These interesting rodents can be observed at twilight. THIS IS A PUBLIC HUNTING AREA; PLEASE CHECK WITH THE MANAGER FOR SEASONS AND AFFECTED AREAS.

Directions: From Charleston, take Exit 58A off Interstate 64 to get onto U.S. Highway 119 south. Travel south on US 119 to the sign for Kanawha State Forest (less than 1 mile), and turn left onto Oakwood Road. After 0.5 mile Oakwood Road makes a sharp left. Turn right onto Bridge Road and go 0.6 mile, then turn right onto Connell Road and travel for 2.1 miles. Turn left onto Kanawha Forest Drive in Loudendale. The forest entrance is 2.4 miles on the right.

Ownership: West Virginia Division of Natural Resources (304) 558-3500

Size: 9,300 acres   **Closest Town:** Charleston

Great blue heron. RON AUSTING PHOTO

REGION THREE: MOUNTAIN LAKES/ MID-OHIO VALLEY

Water is the key to the numerous wildlife viewing opportunities in this region. In the east a series of grand mountain lakes, originally built for flood-control, not only protect West Virginia's residents from floods but provide important aquatic and shoreline habitats for wildlife. In the west, the meandering Ohio River supports some of the richest diversity of freshwater mussels in the United States.

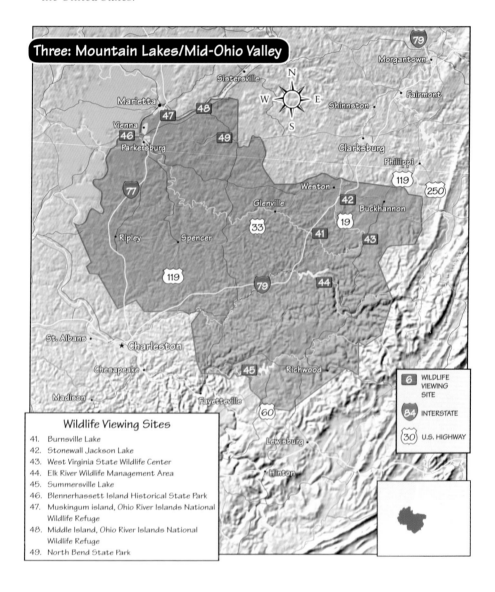

Three: Mountain Lakes/Mid-Ohio Valley

Wildlife Viewing Sites
41. Burnsville Lake
42. Stonewall Jackson Lake
43. West Virginia State Wildlife Center
44. Elk River Wildlife Management Area
45. Summersville Lake
46. Blennerhassett Island Historical State Park
47. Muskingum Island, Ohio River Islands National Wildlife Refuge
48. Middle Island, Ohio River Islands National Wildlife Refuge
49. North Bend State Park

6 WILDLIFE VIEWING SITE

84 INTERSTATE

30 U.S. HIGHWAY

Description: Built for flood control and completed in 1978, the Burnsville Dam not only provided protection for people, but also created 30 miles of shoreline and open water for wildlife. An extensive trail system provides access to more than 12,500 acres of habitat.

Viewing Information: During March and April, search for wild turkeys in the open fields in early morning; look for waterfowl on the lake and ospreys overhead. Summer is best for observing white-tailed deer, red-tailed hawks, and turkey vultures. During winter as many as 1,000 ducks have been seen on this lake, including blacks, mallards, and buffleheads. SOME AREAS ARE OPEN TO HUNTING; PLEASE CHECK WITH THE MANAGER FOR SEASONS AND AFFECTED AREAS.

Directions: *From Interstate 79 take the Burnsville/Glenville exit 79. Travel south toward Burnsville and Burnsville Dam Recreation Area for 0.3 mile to a "T". Turn right and proceed 2.5 miles to the visitor center, on the right. Continue 0.5 mile to the campground, picnic areas, parking lots, and boat ramp.*

Ownership: U.S. Army Corp of Engineers (304) 853-2398 or (304) 853-2371

Size: 968 acres   **Closest Town:** Burnsville

The bufflehead is the smallest of the diving ducks. Differentiate diving ducks like buffleheads from puddle ducks such as mallards and wood ducks by the way they take off from the water. Diving ducks "patter" along the surface before taking off, while puddle ducks spring straight out of the water. RON AUSTING PHOTO

42. STONEWALL JACKSON LAKE

Description: This lake was created in the mid-1980s for flood control and was named after Confederate general Thomas Jonathan "Stonewall" Jackson, who was born in nearby Clarksburg in 1824. This site includes Stonewall Jackson Lake State Park, Stonewall Jackson Lake Wildlife Management Area, and the Stonewall Jackson Dam Area. The 2,650-acre lake is surrounded by gently sloping terrain. Habitats include mixed hardwood forests, old fields, and farmlands reverting to forests.

Viewing Information: Canada geese can be seen year-round on and around the lake; spring and fall are best for other species of waterfowl. In spring, look for ospreys over the lake. The many coves and inlets of this elongated lake provide a haven for great blue herons in spring and summer. White-tailed deer are here year-round. Search the more open forests and fields for wild turkeys. Black bears are present, but are secretive and difficult to see. THIS IS A PUBLIC HUNTING AREA; PLEASE CHECK WITH THE MANAGER FOR SEASONS AND AFFECTED AREAS.

Directions: *Take exit 91 off Interstate 79 and travel south on U.S. Highway 19 for 2.6 miles to the entrance of Stonewall Jackson State Park on the left. Proceed 0.5 mile to the visitor center.*

Ownership: U.S. Army Corp of Engineers (304) 269-4588 or (304) 269-7463; West Virginia Division of Natural Resources (304) 924-6211; West Virginia Division of Parks (304) 269-0523

Size: 2,650 acres   **Closest Town:** Weston

THE MOUNTAIN LAKES

Osprey are often seen over water searching for fish for a meal. The soles of an osprey's feet are equipped with prickly outgrowths that keep slippery fish from sliding away. RON AUSTING PHOTO

43. WEST VIRGINIA STATE WILDLIFE CENTER

Description: Captive native, introduced, and extirpated wildlife of West Virginia can be observed in natural habitat zoological displays. Rooted deep in West Virginia wildlife conservation history, this area was established in 1923 as the French Creek Game Farm to produce game birds and animals for restocking. When the restocking programs were deemed biologically unsound, the state decided to keep wildlife here for educational purposes because the farm was a popular tourist destination. Completely rebuilt in 1984, the facility was renamed the West Virginia State Wildlife Center. Today the center is a state-of-the-art facility operated by the Wildlife Resources Section of the West Virginia Division of Natural Resources.

Viewing Information: Walk the 1.25-mile loop trail to see wildlife that once inhabited the Mountain State, including bison, timber wolves, and mountain lions, as well as two introduced species: European wild boars and ring-necked pheasants. Other native species include white-tailed deer, red and gray foxes, bobcats, raccoons, several species of owls, and many small mammals. Be sure to visit the impressive river otter display, which gives wildlife viewers a rare glimpse into this aquatic mammal's world, from above and below the water.

Directions: At the intersection of West Virginia State Route 4 and WV 20, take WV 20 north 2 miles to the entrance on the east side of WV 20.

Ownership: West Virginia Division of Natural Resources (304) 924-6211

Size: 370 acres   **Closest Town:** Rock Cave

The river otter exhibit is the Wildlife Center's newest exhibit. Otters can be viewed here from both above and below water. RON SNOW PHOTO

Description: This site lies just south of the Elk River and on the east side of Sutton Lake. Fourteen-mile-long Sutton Lake is the result of a dam completed here in 1961 for flood control. The management area's steep hills and ridges are covered in mature hardwood forests and brushlands.

Viewing Information: The level of the lake is controlled by the U.S. Army Corps of Engineers. In the winter, the lake level is lowered 27 feet. White-tailed deer are present year-round. This area offers excellent songbird viewing in spring and summer; Northern cardinals, West Virginia's State bird, live here year-round. Wild turkeys frequently forage in open woods or in clearings, and waterfowl are common on the lake and river. In 1990, 18 male and 10 female river otters were released by the Wildlife Resources Section in the Elk River here in Braxton County as well as in the Elk River southwest of this site in Kanawha County. Look for otters between dawn and midmorning when they are likely to be feeding. THIS IS A PUBLIC HUNTING AREA; PLEASE CHECK WITH THE MANAGER FOR SEASONS AND AFFECTED AREAS.

Directions: *Take the Flatwoods exit 67 off Interstate 79 and travel south on West Virginia State Route 4 for 1.1 miles. Turn left onto WV 15 and proceed to the Holly River Section of the wildlife management area.*

Ownership: U.S. Army Corp of Engineers (304) 765-2816 or (304) 765-2705; West Virginia Division of Natural Resources (304) 924-6211

Size: 18,225 acres   **Closest Town:** Sutton

The cardinal, West Virginia's State bird.
JIM ROETZEL PHOTO

Description: Spectacular rock cliffs and forested hills surround this 2,790-acre lake located 3 miles south of Summersville.

Viewing Information: The public land surrounding this lake is 5,974-acre Summersville Lake Wildlife Management Area. Forest wildlife species are abundant: white-tailed deer, ruffed grouse, and wild turkeys. Canada geese use the lake year-round. Look for ospreys over the lake in spring searching for a meal. In winter black ducks, mallards, and buffleheads frequent the lake. THIS IS A PUBLIC HUNTING AREA; PLEASE CHECK WITH THE MANAGER FOR SEASONS AND AFFECTED AREAS.

Directions: From Summersville, proceed south on U.S. Highway 19 for 3 miles to the entrance, on the right (the sign reads "Summersville Lake/Airport Road"). Proceed 1.7 miles to an intersection where you can turn right to the marina and boat ramp or go straight to the campground.

Ownership: U.S. Army Corp of Engineers (304) 872-5809 or (304) 872-3412

Size: 2,800 acres   **Closest Town:** Summersville

Male ruffed grouse "drum" in the spring to attract females, although drumming can occur throughout the year. The drumming is the sound made as the grouse's wings rapidly beat the air.
LEONARD LEE RUE III PHOTO

Description: Located in the middle of the Ohio River near Parkersburg, the only way to reach Blennerhassett is via a 20-minute sternwheeler ride from Point Park in Parkersburg. The island is a blend of cultural and natural history. It was originally settled in 1798 by Harman Blennerhassett, a wealthy Irishman who built a lavish mansion here only to become involved in a cryptic military operation with Aaron Burr in 1806. Though Burr was acquitted and Blennerhassett released from prison, neither man could return to the life he once knew. No one knows for sure if the men were guilty, although many historians believe there is strong evidence of innocence. The original mansion was burned in 1811 but has since been rebuilt. The 500-acre island is the fifth largest island in the Ohio River.

Viewing Information: The island's 10 miles of shoreline, grassy fields, and marshes provide year-round habitat for numerous species such as white-tailed deer and Canada geese. Bald eagles are present in the spring and ospreys are here in spring and summer. Look for eagles flying overhead. Bald eagles fly with flattened wings, unlike vultures that soar with their wings in a V and ospreys that fly with "bent" wings. Identify eagles at a distance by their great size and wingspan of 7 to 8 feet. Mature birds have characteristic white heads and tails; immature birds are dark all over, although while flying overhead, they show some white underneath their wings. The island is open every weekend from May through October and on Tuesdays through Sundays from May through August.

Directions: *The park museum is located on the corner of Juliana and Second streets near the base of the West Virginia State Route 68 bridge over the Little Kanawha River. Boats leave from a landing on the Ohio River, at the foot of Second Street, 2 blocks from the park museum.*

Ownership: Du Pont; leased and managed by West Virginia Division of Natural Resources, (304) 420-4800

Size: 500 acres   **Closest Town:** Parkersburg

*Bald eagles have been observed harassing ospreys
carrying a fish until the osprey drops the fish,
at which point the eagle seizes it in midair.*

THE MOUNTAIN LAKES

47. MUSKINGUM ISLAND, OHIO RIVER ISLANDS NATIONAL WILDLIFE REFUGE

Description: Like Middle Island (See Site 48), Muskingum Island is one of 19 islands, stretching 362 miles along the Ohio River from Pennsylvania to Kentucky, that make up the Ohio River Islands National Wildlife Refuge. Unlike the more accessible Middle Island, Muskingum is accessible only via a 2-mile boat trip from Williamstown. This island is a mixture of immature and mature bottomland hardwoods, late successional old field openings and sandy beaches. There are scattered large sycamores and cottonwoods on the island; one sycamore has a 22-foot circumference.

Viewing Information: More than 160 species of birds, 40 species of mammals, 50 species of fish, and more than 3 dozen species of mollusks occur in the refuge, many of them on Muskingum Island. The shallow waters of the Ohio support some of the richest diversity of freshwater mussels in the United States: 28 species live here. In summer, search the beach for their discarded shells that have been left by foraging muskrats. Although muskrats are primarily nocturnal they are sometimes seen during the day. Identify a muskrat by its laterally compressed, sparsely haired tail; their dens are large mounds of vegetation. Two of West Virginia's most beautiful warblers nest in the island's interior, one fairly common to the state, and one rare. A small, light blue bird with a black breast band identifies the more common male cerulean warbler; the rarer male prothonotary warbler's head and underside are brilliant yellow. Bank swallows nest on the main channel side of the island. Watch for them as they search for insects over the island's water and fields. Belted kingfishers, great blue herons, and ospreys are also seen from spring to fall. THERE ARE NO COMMERCIAL BOATS TO THIS ISLAND; VIEWERS MUST PROVIDE THEIR OWN BOAT TRANSPORTATION. THIS IS A NATURAL AREA WITH NO FACILITIES AND IT IS A PUBLIC HUNTING AREA; PLEASE CHECK WITH THE MANAGER FOR SEASONS AND AFFECTED AREAS.

Directions: *Access to the island is by boat only. Take Exit 185 off Interstate 77 and travel north 1.4 miles to Williamstown. Turn left onto Riverside Road immediately before the bridge (don't cross bridge). There is a public boat ramp in Williamstown.*

Ownership: U.S. Fish and Wildlife Service (304) 422-0752

Size: 120 acres   **Closest Town:** Williamstown

Bottomland hardwood forest on Muskingum Island. U.S. FISH AND WILDLIFE SERVICE

The Natural Heritage Program of the Wildlife Resources Section conducts an ongoing statewide inventory of rare plant and animal species, wetlands, and other biological communities. The Program identifies unique natural areas and serves as a source for information on the state's natural history. Program information is used to help manage the state's natural resources and minimize the impacts of development on rare plant and animal communities.

48. MIDDLE ISLAND, OHIO RIVER ISLANDS NATIONAL WILDLIFE REFUGE

Description: Middle Island is one of 19 islands that make up the Ohio River Islands National Wildlife Refuge, which stretches 362 miles along the Ohio River from Pennsylvania to Kentucky. Two of the islands are in Pennsylvania, 15 are in West Virginia, and 2 are in Kentucky. One of the most accessible, as well as one of the most beautiful, is Middle Island. A short bridge connects Middle Island with the mainland at St. Marys.

Viewing Information: Middle Island provides some of the best wildlife viewing in the state, and certainly some of the most beautiful river vistas. Throughout the year, wood ducks may be seen in the back channel, and year-round Canada geese nest on the island. Great horned owls are permanent residents; look for them in the mature forest at the head of the island. An active great blue heron rookery on a nearby island increases the chance of seeing one on Middle Island between March and November. Green herons are present in the spring and summer as are belted kingfishers. In May look for bobolinks in the hay fields and adjacent reforested areas. Bald eagles and ospreys are seen occasionally in fall, winter, and spring. In February and March on the main channel search for red-necked grebes. The most common mammals on the island are beavers, cottontail rabbits, muskrats, raccoons, woodchucks, and red foxes. Look for the foxes in spring before the vegetation gets too high and thick. THIS IS A PUBLIC HUNTING AREA; PLEASE CHECK WITH THE MANAGER FOR SEASONS AND AFFECTED AREAS.

Directions: In St. Marys, turn off West Virginia State Route 2 onto George Street and proceed 0.1 mile to the end of street where the bridge connects to Middle Island.

Ownership: U.S. Fish and Wildlife Service (304) 422-0752

Size: 235 acres   **Closest Town:** St. Marys

The Ohio River as seen from Middle Island. R. PHIPPS PHOTO

49. NORTH BEND STATE PARK

Description: North Bend State Park is named for the nearby bend of the North Fork of the Hughes River. For excellent wildlife viewing take the North Bend Rail Trail, a 73-mile recreational trail (hiking and bicycling) running east to west from Parkersburg to Wilsonburg (near Clarksburg). Formerly a rail corridor, it features 13 tunnels and numerous bridges.

Viewing Information: The pastoral landscape of North Bend is ideal white-tailed deer habitat. Deer are browsers and eat twigs, shrubs, grass, herbs, and acorns. During spring and summer, they eat many different types of herbaceous plants, tips of seedlings and shrubs, grasses, elderberries and blackberries, and even mushrooms. In fall, apples, crabapples, and fruits of holly, wild cherries, and greenbrier are favorites. Mast (beechnuts and acorns) fatten them up for the winter. Winter is sometimes hard on deer in West Virginia, especially when heavy snows cover mast, which they "paw" to uncover. When snowcover is heavy they browse on hardwood sprouts and shrubs, rhododendrons, hemlocks, and mountain laurel. Wild turkeys, red and gray squirrels, and eastern chipmunks are common within the park as well. SECTIONS OF THE NORTH BEND TRAIL HAVE NOT BEEN COMPLETED. EXTREME CAUTION SHOULD BE USED IN THESE AREAS. CHECK WITH THE PARK STAFF FOR AFFECTED AREAS.

Directions: *In Parkersburg, take Exit 176 off Interstate 77 and travel east on U.S. Highway 50 for 17.8 miles. Turn right onto WV SR 31 and go south on WV 31, through Cairo, for 4.9 miles. Turn left onto County Route 14 (Low Gap Run Road) and proceed east on CR 14 for 3.2 miles to the park entrance.*

Ownership: West Virginia Division of Natural Resources (304) 643-2931

Size: 1,405 acres   **Closest Town:** Harrisville

THE MOUNTAIN LAKES

Almost all fawns in West Virginia are born between May and July, with most born in June. The white spots serve as camouflage, protecting the fawn from predators. Fawns lose these spots when they are about three months old.

BILL LEA PHOTO

White-tailed deer fawn. BILL LEA PHOTO

REGION FOUR: NORTHERN PANHANDLE/MOUNTAINEER COUNTRY

Reaching deep into Ohio and Pennsylvania, the Northern Panhandle and Mountaineer Country Region is an area of contrasts. Hillcrest Wildlife Management Area, the Mountain State's northernmost wildlife viewing site, is mainly open fields and orchards, while Cathedral State Park, near the eastern border of the region, contains hemlock trees with circumferences in excess of 21 feet. At Cranesville Swamp Nature Preserve, a piece of northern flora continues to thrive from an earlier age, due to the cool microclimate of the area.

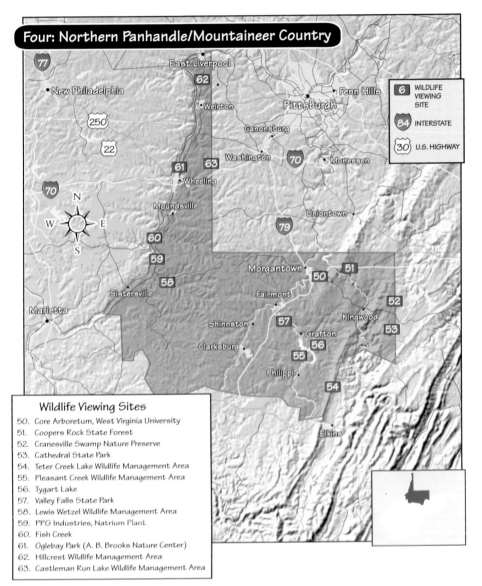

Four: Northern Panhandle/Mountaineer Country

WILDLIFE VIEWING SITE

INTERSTATE

U.S. HIGHWAY

Wildlife Viewing Sites

50. Core Arboretum, West Virginia University
51. Coopers Rock State Forest
52. Cranesville Swamp Nature Preserve
53. Cathedral State Park
54. Teter Creek Lake Wildlife Management Area
55. Pleasant Creek Wildlife Management Area
56. Tygart Lake
57. Valley Falls State Park
58. Lewis Wetzel Wildlife Management Area
59. PPG Industries, Natrium Plant
60. Fish Creek
61. Oglebay Park (A. B. Brooks Nature Center)
62. Hillcrest Wildlife Management Area
63. Castleman Run Lake Wildlife Management Area

Description: Located on the western side of the Evansdale campus of West Virginia University, the Core Arboretum is a teaching and research facility managed by the university's Department of Biology. The arboretum, named after botanist Dr. Earl L. Core, drops 200 feet in elevation from the parking lot to the river. With its varied habitats and location along a major north-flowing river, this site provides numerous wildlife viewing opportunities throughout the year.

Viewing Information: More than 160 species of birds have been seen here. Be sure to obtain a copy of the "Core Arboretum Checklist of Birds" from the Department of Biology. Many species of waterfowl use the river as a resting area during migration, including tundra swans, green-winged teals, northern pintails, ring-necked ducks, lesser scaups, common goldeneyes, buffleheads, red-breasted mergansers, and ruddy ducks. Along the river, especially in quieter areas around the lagoon, look for great blue herons, and in the summer, green herons. Test your identification skills on the 35 species of warblers known to use the arboretum. Bank, barn, and cliff swallows have been recorded recently in the arboretum. The bank swallow is seen during migration, whereas the cliff and barn swallows nest in the state. Several species of woodpeckers are commonly observed. Look for fox squirrels in the more open hardwood sections of the arboretum. Occasionally seen mammals include beavers, muskrats, woodchucks, raccoons, foxes, and deer. THIS IS A NATURAL AREA WITH NO FACILITIES.

Directions: *From Interstate 79, travel south on U.S. Highway 19 (also West Virginia State Route 7) to the West Virginia University Evansdale campus. The Core Arboretum is located on the right 0.1 mile from the coliseum entrance.*

Ownership: West Virginia University Department of Biology (304) 293-5201

Size: 75 acres   **Closest Town:** Morgantown

Barn swallows spend most of their time in the air feeding on insects. Note its deeply forked tail, blue back, and dark cinnamon-buff throat.
BARBARA GERLACH PHOTO

51. COOPERS ROCK STATE FOREST

Description: Just 11 miles east of Morgantown, this state forest offers spectacular views of Cheat River Gorge and miles of hiking trails. It is home to a federally threatened species, the flat-spired three-toothed land snail.

Viewing Information: The flat-spired three-toothed land snail is found only in the Cheat River Gorge of West Virginia. There may be fewer than 500 of these 1-inch mollusks left. If you see fencing in the forest, please respect it; it is protecting important snail habitat. Sixteen trails crisscross this state forest and the adjacent West Virginia University forest, offering wildlife viewers excellent access throughout the two forests. From one of the many Cheat River Gorge overlooks at midday, watch for hawks "kettling," circling and soaring on columns of rising warm air. The land surrounding the archery range is some of the best in the area for viewing songbirds and butterflies in summer. The Virgin Hemlock Trail, which starts at West Virginia State Route 73 leads viewers to a grove of hemlocks that is more than 300 years old. SOME AREAS ARE OPEN TO HUNTING; PLEASE CHECK WITH THE MANAGER FOR SEASONS AND AFFECTED AREAS.

Directions: *From Morgantown, travel east on Interstate 68 for 11 miles to Exit 15. Turn right off the exit ramp and travel 0.3 mile into the park. Once in the park, follow the road 3 miles to the overlook.*

Ownership: West Virginia Division of Natural Resources (304) 594-1561

Size: 12,713 acres   **Closest Town:** Morgantown

The Endangered Species Program of the Wildlife Resources Section is entrusted with the protection and management of rare animals in West Virginia. Fifteen animal species have been listed by the U.S. Fish and Wildlife Service as either threatened or endangered, from the bald eagle to six species of freshwater mussels. Two species, the Cheat Mountain salamander and the flat-spired three-toothed land snail, are found in limited habitats in West Virginia and nowhere else in the world.

Description: Straddling the West Virginia–Maryland border is Cranesville Swamp, a peatland bog formed during the most recent ice age, 15,000 years ago. While most northern species retreated as the climate in the region warmed, a small area of northern flora survived due to the cooler microclimate in this area. The Nature Conservancy has preserved this unique area, which includes the southernmost tamarack forest in the United States. The vegetation is typically Canadian and the preserve boasts 19 distinct plant communities, including sphagnum moss, cranberries, and insectivorous round-leaved sundews.

Viewing Information: The Nature Conservancy maintains four separate trails that provide access to most parts of the preserve. Many mammals inhabit the area, and hikers are likely to see white-tailed deer and possibly a black bear. Wild turkeys inhabit the preserve. The end of May is best for seeing warblers, returning from points south to breed and summer at Cranesville. Hike one of the many trails to see and hear red-eyed vireos back from the Amazon basin in South America, golden-winged warblers back from Guatemala, yellow warblers from Mexico, and hooded warblers from Central America. Northern saw-whet owls nest here, too.

Directions: *From Interstate 68, take the Keyers Ridge exit 14 and travel south on U.S. Highway 219 for 19 miles. South of Deep Creek Lake, turn right off US 219 onto Mayhew Inn Road and go 4 miles. At the stop sign bear left onto Oakland–Sang Run Road and continue for about 0.3 mile. Turn right onto Swallow Falls Road (follow signs for Swallow Falls State Park), and continue for 2.6 miles to a fork. At the fork, turn sharply right onto Cranesville Road. After 4.2 miles, turn left onto Lake Ford Road. Travel on Lake Ford Road for 0.2 mile and turn right at a fork to the preserve entrance, 0.2 mile on the right.*

Ownership: The Nature Conservancy, West Virginia Chapter (304) 345-4350

Size: 1,000 acres   **Closest Town:** Terra Alta

Measuring only eight inches from head to tail, the saw-whet owl is West Virginia's smallest owl. Its name is derived from its call, which sounds like a saw being sharpened.
RON AUSTING PHOTO

53. CATHEDRAL STATE PARK

Description: Although more than 170 species of vascular flora occur here, including 30 tree species, 9 species of ferns, 3 club mosses, and upwards of 50 wildflowers, the centerpiece of this state park is the ancient virgin hemlock forest, with trees towering almost 100 feet high, some with a circumference in excess of 21 feet. The park contains one of the only stands of mixed virgin timber left in the state as well as the largest hemlock in West Virginia. The forest is living testimony to Mr. Branson Haas, a workman at a nearby hotel, who purchased the forest in 1922 and sold it to the state in 1942 with the stipulation the forest never be cut.

Viewing Information: Hike the well-marked Cathedral Trail through the forest and notice how sunlight rarely touches the forest floor. Throughout the year listen and watch for tufted titmice, black-capped chickadees, and red-breasted nuthatches. Identify the chickadee by its *"chick-a-dee-dee-dee"* or *"dee-dee-dee"* and by its black-capped head and black throat. The small gray tufted titmouse has a conspicuous tufted crest and chants *"peter, peter"* over and over. These are social birds, so where one occurs, several others are sure to be around. Identify the red-breasted nuthatch by the conspicuous black line that runs through its eye with a white line above it as it calls a nasal *"yank-yank."* This bird often creeps down one of the large hemlocks head first. Red squirrels and deer mice can also be seen here; like red-breasted nuthatches, they prefer coniferous forests. White-tailed deer, wild turkeys, barred owls, common screech owls, and red and gray foxes may also be observed. Native brook trout can sometimes be seen in the small stream that flows through the area.

Directions: *From the intersection of West Virginia State Route 32 and U.S. Highway 219 in Thomas, travel north on US 219 for 9 miles. Turn left onto WV 24 and go north for 5.5 miles. Turn left onto US 50 and go west for 0.4 mile to the park entrance, on the right.*

Ownership: West Virginia Division of Natural Resources (304) 735-3771

Size: 133 acres   **Closest Town:** Aurora

Aldo Leopold, considered the father of wildlife management in the United States, noted:
"That wildlife is merely something to shoot at or look at is the grossest of fallacies. It often represents the difference between rich country and mere land."

Description: Although small, this is a scenic and diverse wildlife management area. Centered around 35-acre Teter Creek Lake, the area encompasses an oak-hickory forest, shoreline, mixed conifer plantation, and abandoned farmland.

Viewing Information: White-tailed deer and ruffed grouse can be seen here. Several species of amphibians can be seen—and heard—along Teter Creek and the lake; listen for northern spring peepers, one of the earliest signs of spring, beginning in early March. Identification is easy: look for a dark brown X on the back of this small frog's tan body. Songbird viewing is particularly good here, especially around the lake. Bullfrogs and green frogs live here at permanent water sources while the mountain chorus frog is a woodland species. The management area is home to several species of reptiles as well. The abandoned farmlands are excellent for butterfly watching in summer. THIS IS A PUBLIC HUNTING AREA; PLEASE CHECK WITH THE MANAGER FOR SEASONS AND AFFECTED AREAS.

Directions: *From Meadowville, travel east on County Route 9 (Midway/Kirt Road) for 2.6 miles. At the intersection of CR 9 and CR 26 turn right and travel south for 0.2 mile into the wildlife management area.*

Ownership: West Virginia Division of Natural Resources (304) 367-2720

Size: 136 acres   **Closest Town:** Meadowville

The spring peeper is West Virginia's most common frog. RON AUSTING PHOTO

55. PLEASANT CREEK WILDLIFE MANAGEMENT AREA

Description: Pleasant Creek is a broad expanse of marsh surrounded by steep slopes. A bygone farming community, the area contained a grist mill, iron foundry, stores, and a post office. The land was acquired by the federal government to build a flood control dam, resulting in adjacent Tygart Lake. The bottomland in this area is a mixture of willows, hawthorns, sumacs, and alders while the adjacent slopes are a mixed forest of oak, hickory, beech, maple, sassafras, black locust, black birch, and yellow poplar trees. Brushy areas along the upper slopes include hawthorns, blackberries, and raspberries. Intensive management has enhanced the area's value to wildlife: open fields are maintained, trees and shrubs have been planted, and clearings are seeded with grain.

Viewing Information: White-tailed deer, wild turkeys, waterfowl, and many types of songbirds are abundant. Look for Canada geese in early or late winter and in spring on the lake or in the wetlands. Look for beaver or sign of their presence, such as dams and dens: large piles of sticks, twigs, mud, and even small logs across a stream, or large conical mounds of sticks and mud at the water's edge. Although mostly nocturnal, they are sometimes seen during daylight. THIS IS A PUBLIC HUNTING AREA; PLEASE CHECK WITH THE MANAGER FOR SEASONS AND AFFECTED AREAS.

Directions: *From Grafton, travel south on U.S. Highway 119 for 8 miles. Turn left off US 119 onto County Route 119-32 (Pleasant Creek Road) at the wildlife management area sign.*

Ownership: U.S. Army Corp of Engineers (304) 265-1760; West Virginia Division of Natural Resources (304) 457-5144

Size: 3,373 acres   **Closest Town:** Grafton

The beaver is a semiaquatic mammal that feeds on twigs and the soft tissue of bark. JIM ROETZEL PHOTO

56. TYGART LAKE

Description: Built for flood control and completed in 1938, Tygart Dam created 10-mile-long Tygart Lake.

Viewing Information: Tygart Lake is a popular destination for many outdoor recreationists, so get up bright and early when wildlife is the most active and humans aren't. The lake is exceptionally clear and is gaining popularity with snorkelers and scuba divers, especially around Henderson Rocks. Patient divers can glimpse bass, walleyes, muskies, crappies, and perch. The lake's irregular shoreline provides a haven for great blue herons, and the numerous inlets are good for seeing several species of waterfowl: black ducks, mallards, and Canada geese. Look for wood ducks in the quieter inlets and backwater areas. The steep wooded mountainsides along Tygart Lake provide habitat for white-tailed deer, wild turkeys, ruffed grouse, and numerous reptiles and amphibians. In spring, breeding neotropical migratory songbirds fill the woods.

Directions: *From Grafton, take U.S. Highway 50 west 0.3 mile to West Virginia State Route 40 (Riverside Road), which is immediately over the bridge. Turn left onto Riverside Road. Travel 1.9 miles to a "T" and take a right onto Beech Street. Travel another 0.2 mile and turn left onto Walnut Street. After 0.2 mile turn right onto Grand Street, then go 1.9 miles and turn left. Proceed 0.5 mile to the Visitor Center for the Army Corps of Engineers, Tygart Lake. Continue 0.3 mile to the entrance of the state park.*

Ownership: U.S. Army Corp of Engineers (304) 265-1760; West Virginia Division of Natural Resources (304) 265-3383

Size: 1,750 acres   **Closest Town:** Grafton

American black duck. JIM ROETZEL PHOTO

57. VALLEY FALLS STATE PARK

Description: In just 2.5 miles, the river here flows over four waterfalls and 27 rapids. What this small day-use park lacks in size, it more than makes up for in stunning river views, an extensive trail system, and abundant wildlife.

Viewing information: Valley Falls State Park is known for its excellent songbirds. In spring and summer, the forest canopy is active with many neotropical migrants, back from their wintering grounds in the Caribbean and Central and South America. Look for vireos, warblers, and flycatchers in the early morning or evening in the forested areas along the river. White-tailed deer, eastern gray squirrels, and ruffed grouse are abundant. Wild turkeys are also present; the males, known as toms or gobblers, gobble to attract females, called hens, to their breeding grounds. Listen for the familiar gobble in late April when it reaches its peak. Year-round, raccoons can be seen in late evenings. Raccoons are omnivorous and feed on fruits, nuts, bird eggs, crayfish, frogs, and insects.

Directions: *From Interstate 79, take West Virginia State Route 310 (Exit 137 south) for 7.7 miles. Turn right onto County Route 31-14 (Rock Lake–Valley Falls Road) and proceed 0.7 mile. Turn left and go 0.8 mile to the park entrance; the park office is another 0.1 mile on the left. Continue 1 mile to the falls and parking area.*

Ownership: West Virginia Division of Natural Resources (304) 367-2719

Size: 1,145 acres   **Closest Town:** Fairmont

THE NORTHERN PANHANDLE

Willow flycatcher. RON AUSTING PHOTO

Description: Lewis Wetzel was a master woodsman and pioneer who helped settle many parts of West Virginia. Through intensive wildlife management practices such as seeding and planting, the Wildlife Resources Section has improved the quality of the habitat for many species at this area. Oak, hickory, and beech dominate this rugged region, alongside streams, rivers, and ponds.

Viewing Information: Forest species predominate in this management area, including white-tailed deer, wild turkeys, ruffed grouse, raccoons, several species of owls, and songbirds. During summer, Lewis Wetzel WMA is usually quiet. During the day, search the shores of quieter waters for great blue herons. At dusk during the warmer months, watch for bats feeding over small streams and open areas. All of West Virginia's 13 bat species feed on insects. The eastern pipistrelle, red bat, and little brown myotis are found here. It has been reported that the little brown myotis can consume 500 mosquitoes per hour. THIS IS A PUBLIC HUNTING AREA; PLEASE CHECK WITH THE MANAGER FOR SEASONS AND AFFECTED AREAS.

Directions: *From New Martinsville, travel east on West Virginia State Route 7 for 2.7 miles. Turn right onto WV 20 and proceed south for 18.1 miles to Jacksonburg. Turn right onto County Route 82 (Buffalo Run Road) and go south for 3.2 miles. An office with camping information is on the left.*

Ownership: West Virginia Division of Natural Resources (304) 367-2720

Size: 12,498 acres   **Closest Town:** Jacksonburg

More than 90% of West Virginia's wildlife is classified as "nongame." Nongame wildlife are those species which are not hunted, trapped, or fished for. The Wildlife Resources Section's Nongame Wildlife Program's primary responsibility is to conserve the state's wildlife resources through the identification and management of nongame species and their habitats. The program also seeks to inform and educate the public about nongame wildlife.

Description: This is perhaps one of the most unlikely places for a wildlife viewing experience. This site is adjacent to two large chemical plants along the Ohio River and is a prime example of how private businesses can contribute to wildlife education and conservation. The several hundred acres contain an Ohio River backwater area and an extended interface with the forested upland hills and meadows characteristic of this region. The Wildlife Habitat Council recently designated this site as a wildlife management area.

Viewing Information: White-tailed deer, gray and fox squirrels, red and gray foxes, and beavers are present in addition to several flocks of wild turkeys. Early mornings and late evenings are the best for viewing, but it is not unusual to observe many of the species during midday. On summer afternoons pay particular attention to the backwater area, which offers excellent opportunities to see ducks, geese, and a variety of shorebirds. Great blue herons and green herons frequent the marsh areas, and it is not unusual to see an osprey hovering overhead, waiting to turn an unsuspecting fish into a meal.

Directions: *From the intersection of U.S. Highway 250 south and West Virginia State Route 2 in downtown Moundsville, travel south on WV 2 for 17.9 miles to the site, which is between the Pittsburgh Paint and Glass Plant and the Bayer facility.*

Ownership: Pittsburgh Paint and Glass Industries (304) 455-2200

Size: 93 acres   **Closest Town:** New Martinsville

Private industry can also help conserve wildlife habitat.

THE NORTHERN PANHANDLE

60. FISH CREEK

Description: This small day-use area provides panoramic views of the Ohio River.

Viewing Information: During winter, waterfowl frequent the river. Shorebirds are sometimes seen during spring migration and great blue herons are common because there is a rookery on nearby Fish Island. Great blue herons are easily identified by their large size (up to 4 feet tall), long neck and legs, blue-gray color, yellow bill, and white-and-black head. These magnificent birds are usually seen standing at the edge of quieter waters waiting for an unsuspecting fish or frog.

Directions: From the intersection of U.S. Highway 250 south and West Virginia State Route 2 in downtown Moundsville, travel south on WV 2 for 11.3 miles to County Route 27 (Graysville Road). Turn left onto CR 27 and proceed 100 feet to the dirt road on the left. Drive under the bridge to the day-use area.

Ownership: West Virginia Division of Natural Resources

Size: 3 acres　　**Closest Town:** Graysville

61. OGLEBAY PARK (A.B. BROOKS NATURE CENTER)

Description: Oglebay Park is a 1,500-acre park, resort, conference center and home to one of the state's premier nature centers. Oglebay was once the summer estate of Cleveland industrialist Col. Earl Oglebay. This estate was later given to the city of Wheeling for use as a park and recreational area.

Viewing Information: In the summer of 1999, the new $2 million state-of-the-art A.B. Brooks Nature Center opens here. It will feature wildlife, nature, and environmental education exhibits and programs. Visit the nature center and the 15,000-square-foot butterfly and wildflower exhibit or hike along the 4 miles of well-maintained interpretive trails to learn about and view wildlife. This center is well known for its wildlife and environmental education programs for children. Call for details.

Directions: At the intersection of U.S. Highway 40 and West Virginia State Route 88 in Wheeling, travel north on WV 88 for 2.2 miles to the entrance of Oglebay Park.

Ownership: Oglebay Resort and Conference Center (304) 243-4000 or (800) 624-6988

Size: 1,500 acres　　**Closest Town:** Wheeling

Description: Hillcrest is West Virginia's northernmost wildlife management area and consists of flat bottomlands and rolling uplands. The open fields, hedgerows, meadows, and orchards are excellent for viewing wildlife.

Viewing Information: Look for white-tailed deer in the fields in the early morning and evening in summer and in the apple orchards in winter. In spring, come early in the morning to hear ring-necked pheasant cocks crowing, a loud double *"kork-kok,"* or search the hedgerows for these beautiful introduced game birds. Males are easily identified by their large size, long tail, white ring around the neck, and multicolored face. Females are smaller and mottled brown, with a long pointed tail. In spring and summer, the hay fields here support bobolinks and Henslow's sparrows, uncommon birds in West Virginia. Bluebirds also make use of these open fields. In the apple orchard look for Baltimore orioles, meadowlarks, and bluebirds. The fields here in summer are filled with dragonflies and butterflies. In winter, birds of prey migrating down the Ohio River stop at Hillcrest to rest and feed in these same open fields. THIS IS A NATURAL AREA WITH NO FACILITIES AND A PUBLIC HUNTING AREA; PLEASE CHECK WITH THE MANAGER FOR SEASONS AND AFFECTED AREAS.

Directions: *From the junction of U.S. Highway 30 and West Virginia State Route 8 south of Chester, travel south on WV 8 for 2.2 miles to Middle Run Road. Turn left onto Middle Run Road and proceed for 0.9 mile. The area runs along the right and left sides of the road.*

Ownership: West Virginia Division of Natural Resources (304) 367-2720

Size: 1,519 acres   **Closest Town:** Chester

Note the white neck ring, brilliant green head, and pointed tail of this male ring-necked pheasant. Females are mottled brown and lack the beautiful markings of the male. Ring-necked pheasants are natives of southeastern and eastern China and were introduced to the U.S. as a game bird in 1880.
LEONARD LEE RUE III PHOTO

THE NORTHERN PANHANDLE

63. CASTLEMAN RUN LAKE WILDLIFE MANAGEMENT AREA

Description: Castleman Run Lake is surrounded by gently rolling hills and narrow valleys. The bottomlands and forests of this 22-acre lake are mainly sycamore, American elm, sassafras, and black locust.

Viewing Information: Water, woodlands, and open fields are excellent habitats for many species of birds and butterflies during the summer. White-tailed deer are best seen along the forest edge in early morning and evening. Turkeys are abundant and chances of seeing these large birds are good. Listen for the males at dawn and early morning in early spring as they beckon to the females of their harems. THIS IS A PUBLIC HUNTING AREA; PLEASE CHECK WITH THE MANAGER FOR SEASONS AND AFFECTED AREAS.

Directions: *Travel west on West Virginia State Route 67 from Bethany until just outside of town, about 0.2 mile. Turn right onto County Route 32; this intersection is not marked and is before the soccer field. Travel south on CR 32 for 3.5 miles to the lake.*

Ownership: West Virginia Division of Natural Resources (304) 367-2720

Size: 343 acres   **Closest Town:** Bethany

White-tailed buck deer. BILL LEA PHOTO

WILDLIFE INDEX

This listing represents some of the more popular species in West Virginia, as well as some of the best places to see them. This is only a partial list. The numbers following each species are site numbers, not page numbers.

Discover the Thrill of Watching Wildlife.

 The Watchable Wildlife® Series

Published in cooperation with Defenders of Wildlife, these high-quality, full color guidebooks feature detailed descriptions, side trips, viewing tips, and easy-to-follow maps. Wildlife viewing guides for the following states are now available with more on the way.

Alaska
Arizona
California
Colorado
Florida
Idaho
Indiana
Iowa
Kentucky

Massachusetts
Montana
Nebraska
Nevada
New Hampshire
New Jersey
New Mexico
New York
North Carolina
North Dakota
Ohio

Oregon
Puerto Rico &
  Virgin Islands
Tennessee
Texas
Utah
Vermont
Virginia
Washington
West Virginia
Wisconsin

Watch for this sign along roadways. It's the official sign indicating wildlife viewing areas included in the Watchable Wildlife® Series.

■ *To order any of these books, check with your local bookseller or call FALCON at* 1-800-582-2665.

www.FalconOutdoors.com

FALCON®